The Journey to Discover "GOD, the Holy Spirit"

By D. Michael Cotten

Cover Photo by John Cunyus
Contact the Author at
dmichaelcotten@att.net

Searchlight Press
Who are you looking for?
Publishers of thoughtful Christian
books since 1994.
PO Box 554
Henderson, TX 75653-0554
www.JohnCunyus.com

Premise
How do we love GOD for who GOD is?

Believers must not accept as entitlement, GOD and His Creation, or Jesus and His redemption, or "GOD, the Holy Spirit". There is a destiny for every Believer that requires faith in GOD to attain. If you can meet your destiny with your own ability you have not found your true destiny. Believers must understand that Jesus died to make Believers righteous, so the Believers would qualify to receive "GOD, the Holy Spirit" to abide inside Believers. If Believers do not communicate with and accept leadership from "GOD, the Holy Spirit", Believers wasted their inheritance from Jesus Christ.

Believers, who are redeemed, are not your own, having been purchased by Jesus Christ. Listen to these scriptures to begin to understand your position in the world.
> • Have ye not known that your body is a sanctuary of the Holy Spirit in you, which ye have from God? and you are not your own, for ye were bought with a price; glorify, then, God in your body and in your spirit, which are God's. 1st Corinthians 6:19-20
> • For by grace are ye saved through faith; and that not of yourselves: it is the gift of God: Ephesians 2:8
> • We now have the very highest of all callings, as children of God, and we must "walk worthy of our calling". Ephesians 1:4
> • And a person's enemies will be those of his own

household. Whoever loves father or mother more than me is not worthy of me, and whoever loves son or daughter more than me is not worthy of me. And whoever does not take his cross and follow me is not worthy of me. Whoever finds his life will lose it, and whoever loses his life for my sake will find it. Matthew 10:36

Until Believers realize your only destiny is to love GOD for who GOD is, His Son for the redemption of Believers, the gift of "GOD, the Holy Spirit", and others more significantly than yourself, the Believer is caught up with selfaggrandizement. Believers, who do not operate in love for GOD and others will flounder in idolatry of "me and mine" and live in man-made outcomes or consequences. Everyone whoever loved GOD, from the beginning of time to the end of time, was saved by the blood of Jesus Christ who reconciled the world to GOD. Rejection of Jesus Christ as your Savior will cause your name to be blotted out of the "Lamb's Book of Life".

Table of Contents

Words from the Author about Writing Style

This book is not written in strict adherence to grammatical rules. The Bible and concepts of GOD are complicated. To unpack the compound sentences and the interaction of the visible and invisible world; each page will contain highlights, capital letters, quotes, underlines and cascading verses, to add sound and definition to the words.

Treatment of the Name of "GOD, the Holy spirit"

The Holy Spirit's name is not Holy Spirit, but is "GOD, the Holy Spirit" we serve one God in three aspects: Father GOD, Jesus Christ, our Redeemer, and "GOD, the Holy Spirit". In this book the name, Holy Spirit, will be changed to reflect the full name "GOD, the Holy Spirit" to remind believers of who is living inside Believers and the incomparable power that is "GOD, the Holy Spirit".

I am He who created you.
Foundational Truth #1

GOD gave mankind all power over everything on the earth, above the earth, and below the seas in Genesis, in addition GOD gave man a free will to act as mankind is pleased to act, so when there is a discussion of GOD chastening his creation, the chastening must comply with the parameters GOD has set for Himself. For example, there is very little room in the 23rd Psalm for GOD to chasten His children who follow His leadership.

Final conclusion; Believers and unbelievers reap the evil they sew by choosing to be led away from GOD's instructions, when Believers come back to the love available from GOD and the total wellbeing offered by GOD's leadership they are welcomed like the prodigal son.

GOD does not have to chasten mankind, mankind when acting on the negative side of GOD's instructions, receive what GOD said happens when mankind is not being led by GOD and his instructions.

Here is a list of principles and scriptures that will keep Believers stretching for the high prize of relationship with GOD, Almighty.

> 1. Life of prayer Mark 1:35-37 You cannot live a godly life without constant communication with GOD.
> 2. Trust in GOD Proverbs 3:5 What is not of faith is sin.
> 3. Meditate on GOD's word and strive for Intimacy with GOD. Isaiah 43:1-3

4. Obedience to GOD and His instructions Deuteronomy 28:1-3 You must choose life or suffer death.

5. Depending on "GOD, the Holy Spirit" moment by moment. Ephesians 5:18, Acts 1:8 Jesus died to give you "GOD, the Holy Spirit" for comfort, peace, and power.

6. Consider GOD and others more significantly than yourself. Mark 12:33 Those who do not love, do not know GOD, for GOD is love.

7. Live with a forgiving heart for GOD owns everything and everyone. Matthew 6:12-15 You were bought with a heavy price.

Isaiah 43:1-3 But now thus says the LORD, he who created you, O Jacob, he who formed you, O Israel: "Fear not, for I have redeemed you; I have called you by name, you are mine. When you pass through the waters, I will be with you; and through the rivers, they shall not overwhelm you; when you walk through fire you shall not be burned, and the flame shall not consume you. **For I am the LORD your God, the Holy One of Israel, your Savior.**

Do you believe GOD is who He said He is?
Foundational Truth #2

The Lord's blood has been presented in Heaven at the Holy of Holies and the devil's authority to accuse the brethren was taken away by GOD Almighty. Believers have been restored to right-standing with GOD Almighty through Jesus Christ and the Lord's authority on earth has been returned to Believers. Watch closely to the following scriptures and follow the Lord's ascension to Heaven to present the Lord's blood and resurrected saints for the First Fruits offering in Heaven. Then the Ancient of Days or Father GOD gave Jesus authority, glory, dominion, and an everlasting Kingdom to Jesus and judged the Devil, and victory to the Believers.

Adam and Eve gave Satan
their dominion over the earth.

Luke 4:6 And the Devil said to Jesus, All this power I will give you, and the glory of them; for it has been delivered to me. And I give it to whomever I will.

Jesus announces He will restore mankind to GOD
and bring judgement on the Devil.

John 12:30-32 Jesus answered, "This voice has come for your sake, not mine. Now is the judgment of this world; **now** will the ruler of this world be cast out. And I, when I am lifted up from the earth, will draw all people to myself."

In a little while I will go
and in a little while return to you.

God, the Holy Spirit, 9

John 14:15-20 If ye love me, keep my commandments. And I will pray the Father, and he shall give you another Comforter, that he may abide with you for ever; Even the Spirit of truth; whom the world cannot receive, because it seeth him not, neither knoweth him: but ye know him; for he dwelleth with you, and shall be in you. I will not leave you comfortless: **I will come to you. Yet a little while,** and the world seeth me no more; **but ye see me:** because I live, ye shall live also. At that day ye shall know that I am in my Father, and ye in me, and I in you.

**Jesus will go away and
Jesus will come again to you in a little while.**

John 14:25-29 These things have I spoken unto you, being yet present with you. **But the Comforter, which is the Holy Ghost, whom the Father will send in my name,** he shall teach you all things, and bring all things to your remembrance, whatsoever I have said unto you. Peace I leave with you, my peace I give unto you: not as the world giveth, give I unto you. Let not your heart be troubled, neither let it be afraid. **Ye have heard how I said unto you, I go away, and come again unto** you. If ye loved me, ye would rejoice, because I said, **I go unto the Father**: for my Father is greater than I. And now I have told you before it come to pass, that, when it is come to pass, ye might believe. (No one will have a problem knowing Jesus second coming)

**Your Sorrow Will Turn into Joy
When You See Jesus After Resurrection**

Joh 16:16-18 "A little while, and you will see me no longer; and again a little while, and you will see me." So some of his disciples said to one another, "What is this that he says to us, 'A little while, and you will not see me, and again a little while, and you will see me'; and, 'because I am going to the Father'?"

John 16:20 Truly, truly, I say to you that you will weep and lament, but the world will rejoice. And you will be sorrowful, but your sorrow shall be turned into joy....John 16:22 And therefore you now have sorrow. But I will see you again, and your heart will rejoice, and no one will take your joy from you.

Jesus preaches in Hell
during the three days in the tomb.

Matthew 12:40 For as Jonas was three days and three nights in the whale's belly; **so shall the Son of man be three days and three nights in the heart of the earth.**

Ephesians 4:8-10 Wherefore he saith, When he ascended up on high, **he led captivity captive, and gave gifts unto men.** (Now that he ascended, what is it but that he also descended first into the lower parts of the earth? He that descended is the same also that ascended up far above all heavens, that he **might fill all things.)**

Jesus preached in Hell
to the people lost before the flood.

1st Peter 3:18-20 For Christ also suffered once for sins,

the righteous for the unrighteous, that he might bring us to God, being put to death in the flesh but made alive in the spirit, in which he (Christ) <u>went and proclaimed to the spirits in prison</u>, **because they formerly did not obey, when God's patience waited in the days of Noah,** while the ark was being prepared, in which a few, that is, eight persons, were brought safely through water.

Jesus takes the keys to Hell
and death when he leaves Hell.

Revelation 1:17-18 ... Fear not; I am the first and the last: I am he that liveth, and was dead; and, behold, I am alive for evermore, Amen; and **have the keys of hell and of death.**

The sins of the world are forgiven and forgotten
for those that believe and choose
Jesus as Lord of their life.

Colossians 2:13-15 And you, being dead in your sins and the uncircumcision of your flesh, hath he quickened together with him, **having forgiven you all trespasses; Blotting out the handwriting of ordinances that was against us,** which was contrary to us, and took it out of the way, **nailing it to his cross;** And <u>having spoiled principalities and powers, he made a shew of them openly, triumphing over them in it.</u>

**Saints were resurrected and went to Heaven
with Jesus when He ascended to the Father
for the First Fruits offering.**

Matthew 27:50-54 And Jesus **cried out again with a loud voice and yielded up his spirit.** And behold, the curtain of the temple was torn in two, from top to bottom. And the earth shook, and the rocks were split. <u>The tombs also were opened</u>. **And many bodies of the saints who had fallen asleep were raised, and coming out of the tombs after Jesus resurrection they went into the holy city and appeared to many (These saints were the first fruits of the resurrection presented to the Father with the Blood of the Lamb by Jesus Christ.).** When the centurion and those who were with him, keeping watch over Jesus, **saw the earthquake and what took place, they were filled with awe and said, "Truly this was the Son of God!"**

**Jesus appears to Mary Magdalene
but won't allow her to touch Him
until He returns from ascending to the Father.**

John 20:14-17 And when she had thus said, she turned herself back, and saw Jesus standing, and knew not that it was Jesus. Jesus saith unto her, Woman, why weepest thou? whom seekest thou? She, supposing him to be the gardener, saith unto him, Sir, if thou have borne him hence, tell me where thou hast laid him, and I will take him away. Jesus saith unto her, Mary. She turned herself, and saith unto him, Rabboni; which is to say, Master.

Jesus saith unto her, **Touch me not;** for **I am not yet ascended to my Father: but go to my brethren, and say unto them, I ascend unto my Father, and your Father; and to my God, and your God.**

On the first day of the week and the Day of First Fruits, Jesus ascends to Heaven and returns to appear to the Disciples, the same day.

John 20:19-23 **Then the same day at evening,** being the first day of the week, when the doors were shut where the disciples were assembled for fear of the Jews, came Jesus and stood in the midst, and saith unto them, Peace be unto you. And when he had so said, **he shewed unto them his hands and his side. Then were the disciples glad,** when they saw the Lord. Then said Jesus to them again, Peace be unto you: as my Father hath sent me, even so send I you. And when he had said this, he breathed on them, and saith unto them, **Receive ye the Holy Ghost:** Whose so ever sins ye remit, they are remitted unto them; and whose soever sins ye retain, they are retained.

Jesus presents the resurrected saints and His sinless blood to the Father as fulfillment of the "First Fruits offering".

Hebrews 9:11-12 But when Christ appeared as a high priest of the good things that have come, then through the greater and more perfect tent (not made with hands, that is, not of this creation) **he entered once for all into**

the holy places, not by means of the blood of goats and calves but **by means of his own blood, thus securing an eternal redemption.**

The Ancient of Days Reigns
Restores the authority to Believers.

Daniel 7:9-12 I beheld till the thrones were cast down, and the Ancient of days did sit, whose garment was white as snow, and the hair of his head like the pure wool: his throne was like the fiery flame, and his wheels as burning fire. A fiery stream issued and came forth from before him: thousand thousands ministered unto him, and ten thousand times ten thousand stood before him: the judgment was set, and the books were opened. I beheld then because of the voice of the great words which the horn spake: I beheld even till **the beast** was slain, and his body destroyed, and given to the burning flame. As concerning the rest of the beasts, **they had their dominion taken away:** yet their lives were prolonged for a season and time. (the devil's power and sin was atoned)

The Son of Man Is Given Dominion
And taken away from Satan.

Daniel 7:13-14 I saw in the night visions, and, behold, **one like the Son of man came with the clouds of heaven** (resurrected saints and blood of the Lamb), and came to the Ancient of days, and they brought him near before him. And **there was given (Jesus)** him dominion, and glory, and a kingdom, that all people, nations, and languages, should serve him: **his dominion is an everlasting dominion, which shall not pass away, and his kingdom that which shall not be destroyed.**

The Saints are judged victorious over the Devil
and dominion in the earth was restored.

Daniel 7:21-22 I watched, and that horn made war with the saints and overcame them until the **Ancient of Days came, and judgment was given to the saints of the Most High.** And the time came that the saints possessed the kingdom.

Jesus returning dominion to Believers
and assigning the great commission.

Matthew 28:18-20 And Jesus came and said to them, **"All authority in heaven and on earth has been given to me.** Go therefore and make disciples of all nations, baptizing them in the name of the Father and of the Son and of the Holy Spirit, teaching them to observe all that I have commanded you. And behold, **I am with you always, to the end of the age."**

The giving of "GOD, the Holy Spirit"
started the New Covenant
and the Church era with GOD.

John 14:26 But the Comforter, which is the Holy Spirit, **whom the Father will send in my name, he shall teach you all things, and bring all things to your remembrance,** whatsoever I have said unto you.

The Journey to discover "GOD, the Holy Spirit"

Chapter 1

The old Covenants are between GOD and Mankind.
The New Covenant is between Father GOD and Jesus.

GOD has always dealt with mankind with agreements and covenants. Let us look at the covenant made between GOD and Israel to understand the **"old system"** with GOD; that if you do good, you get good and if you do bad, you get bad. **GOD gave Israel the "If you do" blessings and "if you do not" curses in Deuteronomy 28. Jesus redeemed Believers from the curses of mankind's inability to keep the law, so that the New Covenant Believers are free from the curses, only the blessings remain.**
The new Covenant is not with GOD and mankind, or GOD and Israel, but **the New Covenant is with and between Father GOD and Jesus Christ;** that is why the New Covenant has worked and why there is awesome power in the gospel of Jesus Christ.
Jesus lived under the covenant of the Law,
Died, and was resurrected so that
Believers do not have to live
under the covenant of the Law.

After all the failures of mankind being unfaithful with GOD, Father GOD made the New Covenant with Himself and Jesus because Mankind is not faithful, and Jesus was perfectly faithful. **NOW, Believers can live in the**

faithfulness of Jesus Christ. Each Believer's faith must be in the faithfulness of Jesus. Do you see the difference? Believers do not have to depend **on our faith** but on the faith of Jesus Christ and Father GOD. Believers know that each and every promise of the Lord is actionable, because Jesus was faithful. Listen to the promise.

Galatians 2:20 I have been crucified with Christ. It is no longer I who live, but Christ who lives in me. And the life I now live in the flesh **I live by faith of the Son of God,** who loved me and gave himself for me.

Mark 11:22-26 And Jesus answering saith unto them, Have faith in God. For verily I say unto you, That whosoever shall say unto this mountain, Be thou removed, and be thou cast into the sea; and shall not doubt in his heart, but shall believe that those things which he saith shall come to pass; he shall have whatsoever he saith. Therefore I say unto you, What things soever ye desire, when ye pray, believe that ye receive *them,* and ye shall have *them.*

2nd Peter 1:2 Grace and peace be multiplied unto you **through the knowledge of God, and of Jesus our Lord,** According as his divine power hath given unto us all things that pertain unto life and godliness, through the knowledge of him that hath called us to glory and virtue: Whereby are given unto us **exceeding great and precious promises:** that by these ye might be **partakers of the divine nature,** having escaped the corruption that is in the world through lust.

Did you see; "I live by Faith of the Son of GOD". Many translations translate Faith "of" the Son of GOD to faith "in" the Son of GOD. It is more factual, literal, and logical **to have faith in the faith of Jesus Christ** who accomplished the acts of kindness Jesus saw Father GOD do and say. Believing in the faith of Jesus to do a mighty work to bring glory to your Savior and GOD is easier than believing you can with human power do anything. Remember Jesus said he could do nothing without the Father and the same goes for Believers we need "GOD, the Holy Spirit" to partner with us to do the things GOD wants to do through Believers.

Now let us add some logic; The world of the Old Covenant, Jesus lived under, included all the curses from Deuteronomy 28 which have been nailed to the cross with our sins and punishment, leaving only the blessings, right-standing with GOD, and the gift of "GOD, the Holy Spirit". Believers are living in a different world with new promises, a New Covenant, a devil stripped of his kingdoms, and an advocate with GOD Almighty who has felt what Believers have felt without sinning.

Listen to the Apostle Paul describe the awesome position of Believers in Christ Jesus through the Lord's Holy Spirit.

> **Ephesians 3:14-19** For this reason I bow my knees before the Father, **from whom every family in heaven and on earth is named,** that according to the riches of his glory he may grant you to be strengthened with power **through his Spirit in your inner being,** so that Christ may dwell in your

hearts through faith—that you, being rooted and grounded in love, **may have strength to comprehend with all the saints what is the breadth and length and height and depth, and to know the love of Christ that surpasses knowledge, that you may be filled with all the fullness of God.**

The humility of realizing your place in GOD's family will allow GOD to give you **the "desires** of your heart" for pleasing your Father GOD and your redeemer Jesus Christ. Acts of kindness completed in partnership with "GOD, the Holy Spirit" is the most fulfilling of all desires. Trying to be great in the eyes of your peers and gaining inferior notoriety is a failing gesture, when you can be a son or daughter of the Most-High GOD.

Elements of your New Creation Spirit.

> The Lord has made your Spirit perfect and abides inside Believers.
>
> The Lord remembers your sins no longer.
>
> The Lord gives mercy for your lawlessness.
>
> The Lord's grace is there for everything you do for others.
>
> GOD gave you "the mind of Christ" to use on Earth to benefit others.
>
> Believers can depend on the faith of Jesus, not their own faith.
>
> Believers can now speak forth the word of GOD and expect the words to change the very make-up of the seen world.
>
> Believers are only limited by the size of your

relationship with GOD and the motivation of your heart.

Believers must live in the confidence of these promises from GOD or you will live without your true identity in Christ Jesus. Did you notice all these promises are in the past tense, they are finished works of your Savior, Father, and Holy Spirit of GOD?

**God is the reality and
the shiny things are a lie.**

GOD provided the promises and the sacrifice of Jesus Christ to make us righteous in our Spirit so that Believers would qualify for receiving the gift of "GOD, the Holy Spirit", the blessings of Abraham, and take away the curses of the law. Believers have inherited a supernatural world **only limited by your knowledge, belief, and relationship with "GOD, the Holy Spirit".**

> **2nd Peter 1:1-2** ...To those who have obtained a faith of equal standing with ours by the righteousness of our God and Savior Jesus Christ: May grace and peace be multiplied to you **in the knowledge of God and of Jesus our Lord.**

The enemy of your faith will try to undermine your identity in Jesus Christ and your status as a child of GOD by seeding thoughts of unworthiness and condemnation to dim your belief. **Remember,** the Lord does not tempt nor condemn Believers, so gear up against the devil and protect your mind and brain. (James 1:13) Constantly beware of temptations to follow what is popular, or in style, or in vogue and **capture those thoughts and expel them from your brain.** Believers cannot do anything to earn GOD's favor but are expected to take authority over their thought life and act with kindness to others.

There are warnings throughout the Bible about keeping your heart right with GOD. The grace of GOD is a gift and you do not have to work for it, just **Believe and act on the promises with the leading of "GOD, the Holy Spirit". Listen to the Apostle Peter.**

> **2nd Peter 3:8** You therefore, **beloved,** knowing this beforehand, **take care** that you are not carried away with the error of lawless people and **lose your own stability.** But grow in **the grace and knowledge of our righteousness in our Savior, Jesus Christ.**

Believers must avoid being a part of the worldly system and influenced by demonic forces that tempt Believers. Believers must capture chaotic thoughts to keep them from becoming mindsets in the brain and disrupting the Believers relationship with GOD. Remember the three sins that GOD hates; The lust of the flesh, lust of the eye, and the pride of life come from thoughts that can and should be stopped and thrown out of your brain. Just as the Lord, thwarted the tempting of the Devil, with the word of GOD, Believers must have the word of GOD stored in our hearts to thwart temptations, from the enemy.

Listen to this warning from GOD in Jeremiah.

> **Thus says the LORD:** "Let not the wise man boast in his wisdom, let not the mighty man boast in his might, let not the rich man boast in his riches, **but**

let him who boasts boast in this, that he understands and knows (is intimate with Me) me, that I am the LORD who practices steadfast love, justice, and righteousness in the earth. For in these things I delight, declares the LORD."
Jeremiah 9:23

Humility is the key for Believer's lives and it is not difficult to be humble when Believers understand what GOD has accomplished in His creation including the creation of the world and our bodies. When Believers cast their care on "GOD, the Holy Spirit" and consult for a daily plan, the Believer is in the right position for the blessing and provision of GOD.

Think about this; All Believers accomplishments have been accomplished, using something GOD created. Not one thing has been invented or discovered that GOD did not make the core building blocks. Inventors and scientists are working with things GOD created; for example, the I-phone uses airwaves and soundwaves that were discovered from GOD's creation, the satellites stay in their positions because of gravity. Even the bats are flying around using GOD's radar system (the first GPS system). The arrogant are prideful and boast of their accomplishments instead of acknowledging, what they have discovered about GOD's Creation, with their mind, that GOD also created.

The <u>unbeliever</u> or doubter's own pride may say, "I don't need GOD I have plenty of money and houses and supply for my family." That pride will keep unbelievers and doubters living in their own power and supply. Think about it; **without acknowledging and honoring GOD and His creation, the Believer will be controlled by pride in his accomplishments.** This attitude is very short sighted, there will be needs successful people cannot supply, for example, peace, salvation, health, and deliverance. What will the successful man do when he or she needs GOD and you don't know where GOD is or how to communicate with GOD?

Most Christians have not realized Father GOD's relationship with His creation and world; and do not understand **the Believer's position in GOD's World?** GOD has a total commitment to loving mankind and the world GOD created for His love child. The love is so deep that Father GOD gave His only Son for mankind for all who would believe. That is the love expressed and acted on by GOD for you. If you measured the size of your relationship with GOD in the amount of time you spend with GOD; **how large is the timeshare of your relationship with GOD?**
Plant this thought in your imagination, if GOD had a cell phone, your face would be the screen saver and your number would be on speed dial, signifying your importance to GOD. What is your response to GOD, for His love for you and His desire to talk to and be a part of your day, every day? You can return GOD's love and live inside His provision, leadership, blessing, and inclusion in GOD's family or you can choose to live unto yourself and not bother. **Remember** "GOD, the Holy Spirit" is waiting

for you to walk into a room of people or family and ask if GOD has a "word of knowledge" for someone in the room that will change their life.

God will not share his glory with you; if you work to be your sufficiency, GOD rests and if you rest in GOD's sufficiency, GOD supplies your needs according to His riches. The Christian life is about relationship with a loving GOD; GOD will be with you when there is problem but GOD desires to be there with Believers **before there is a problem,** *so that GOD can guide you away from problems.* Constantly remember everything "born" out of your relationship with GOD is divinely inspired and supplied.

Consider the problems of thinking you are a self-made man:

- The **first problem** of being accomplished at your job, a good breadwinner for your family, and even being a good member of a church; your personal accomplishments do not measure your commitment to GOD. Being a better person than some others at church is failed thinking.
- The **second problem** of being successful in supplying your needs in the world, is that your accomplishments **do not** reveal the part, God played in creating those parts of your life.
- The **third problem** of being successful; is success offers **no** understanding of how to solve a spiritual problem or to aspire to a spiritual objective.

- The **fourth problem** of success is happiness and fulfillment **cannot** come from your senses but must be from the heart and from the Spiritual realm. Peace comes from a pure conscience and joy from the heart of the redeemed.

A Believer, who does not have a pure conscience or a heart full of the joy is not living the abundant life Jesus died to give Believers. Believers depending on their own abilities, have lost, momentarily, connection with the love of GOD. Think about being well off with the blessing of GOD or mired in the never-ending pursuit to provide for yourself.

Proverbs 10:22 The blessing of the LORD makes rich, **and he (GOD) adds no sorrow with it.**

1. You are not rich, if you have money in the bank and are dying of cancer. That is not rich.

2. If you live in a wonderful home and are depressed, you are not truly rich.

3. If you have riches but your children are addicted to drugs, you are not rich.

The blessing of the Lord makes rich and GOD adds no sorrow with the riches. Therefore, negative situations **are not from the Lord;** bad results are man-made and lack GOD's grace. Bad results are not in your life to teach you something, bad results are man-made and not the product of blessings, but of curses if they add sorrow. **Believers can learn from every situation,** but it is better to live in concert with "GOD, the Holy Spirit" and be in situations that are "born" out of your relationship with

God, the Holy Spirit, 26

GOD. **The essence of the Lord's love for you, begs you to come to "GOD, the Holy Spirit" to plan your day. The Believers act of coming to GOD for direction will show your love and respect for GOD and great things will be born out of your love for GOD and GOD's love for you.**

Let us dissect planning our day and problem resolution; Faith through grace with love is the combination that produce divine outcomes, but what does that mean? Believers must have an intimate relationship with GOD to mix the grace of GOD with the Believers faith in GOD's word to produce divine outcomes.   If, as Believers, we are fighting the curses of the law, we have mixed faith in GOD with faith in ourselves and that stifles a Believers access to GOD's grace on the Believers timetable. Jesus explains in 1st Peter 5:7 Believers should not harbor the care and be upset and try to make a man-made plan but instead bring it to "GOD, the Holy Spirit" for a spiritual plan.

Scripture from the Lord reveals.

> **"Cast your care (anxiety) on Jesus for He cares (is in charge of eradicating problems) for you." 1st Peter 5:7**

The first word "care" in the scripture is for things that are bothering you and the second word "cares" is melo in the Greek language meaning; is responsible for or distributes to the needed or eradicates).

The most important take away from this promise is the constancy of giving your cares to the grace of GOD through communication with "GOD, the Holy Spirit"

because GOD cares for you.

**How can a successful Believer
stay in proper relationship with GOD?**

The first answer to the problem of being successful in the world and staying in an intimate relationship with GOD.

Acknowledge the GOD of Creation for everything created and acknowledge and honor GOD, who has given you the ability to get wealth. There is **no thing** that you use in your occupation to supply your needs, that GOD did not make. Take a minute to think about that fact. In addition, to supplying Believers needs, GOD made the beauty of growing things like flowers and trees, lakes and mountains, and oceans and rivers for your pleasure.

The second answer to the problem of being successful in the world and staying in proper relationship with GOD.

Are you working for things that you can't take to Heaven and why? Get wisdom and the understanding of GOD, because without knowledge of GOD and His word you cannot understand the Spiritual world and the power to deal with spiritual problems, health, happiness, and eternal life.

The third answer to the problem of being successful in the world and staying in loving relationship with GOD.

Be consumed with seeking a relationship with

God, the Holy Spirit, 28

Jesus Christ and "GOD, the Holy Spirit", without the Holy Spirit you are no match for the devil.

The fourth answer to the problem of being successful in the world and staying in proper relationship with GOD:

Do not be confused, the riches of this world **will not** bring joy, fulfillment, peace, or Godliness. You cannot buy your way into heaven, or curse cancer in your body, or cast depression into the sea, or receive anything from GOD without a relationship with Jesus Christ and "GOD, the Holy Spirit".

The fifth answer to the problem of being successful and keeping a proper relationship with GOD.

Do not procrastinate, you will miss your destiny that God made for you to accomplish. You will never be happier than when you are accomplishing a task given you, by Almighty GOD. There are people in your life who need an act of kindness or salvation from Jesus and **your life is the sermon they are hearing. Your life can influence others to want a loving, caring, and eternal relationship with Jesus Christ.**

A Believer cannot take any part of your success on earth to Heaven, so what is Earthly success worth in Eternity.

I recently saw an interview with Tim Tebow and was amazed; a brief compilation of the interview is below:

He was a remarkable youth athlete.

He won the Heisman Trophy,

He was made fun of for being a Christian,

He was given a lucrative contract to play football,

He was not as successful as he hoped in football,

GOD prospered Tim in his life and other business, He has a platform to help people and is active with his kindness,
He was very successful at helping people and living for GOD,
He was 31 and was not going to have sex until he found Miss Universe.
He literally found Miss Universe helping children at a charity event.
They fell in love and are to be married.
They love each other and they love GOD and helping others.
People say He was an incomplete quarterback for the NFL.

Other people will say, live your life" like Tim Tebow, loving GOD with all your heart, mind, soul, and strength and loving your neighbor as yourself.

I was overwhelmed by his commitment to GOD and to the success of a committed life in partnership with "GOD, the Holy Spirit". Everything about Tim exuded happiness and a successful life in GOD, success in football is not everything, it's not even in the top ten. Tim was humble and inspirational to me and I can only hope that someone might say of me, "he was committed to GOD with everything in him". GO Tim Tebow.

Create images of GOD abiding in the Temple in your body And you abiding with "GOD, the Holy Spirit".

Living with the power of the Kingdom of God, inside

Believers, right now, on earth; is exciting and desirable. In contrast, self-centered pursuits are empty and do not offer salvation, wisdom, redemption, justification and all the benefits of a relationship with Jesus Christ.

Listen to words describing the Believer's inheritance from just one scripture.

> **1st Corinthians 1:30** But of him are ye in Christ Jesus, who of God is made unto us (Believers) **wisdom,** and **righteousness,** and **sanctification,** and **redemption:**

Do you have a vision or an image in your mind and heart of these four Bible words? Stop reading the Bible when you do not understand a word, principle, or context and **investigate.** After analyzing, create images in your heart; to detail and strengthen your faith in the gifts GOD has given you in the inheritance from Jesus Christ. Let us go over these words and their meanings again; **Imagine the benefits of being a Believer, you are righteous, you are sanctified, you are redeemed, and you have the Lord's wisdom available.** If these words don't create an image of the power of right standing with GOD and the love of your Savior, you must reprogram your mind and picture bank. If the answer to this question; is you don't have a good understanding of these four words, this needs immediate attention. Develop for yourself 3D pictures of these words so that these words have the power GOD installed in them to fulfill their meaning when GOD inspired the writers of the Bible to write them.

- **Justified:** Just-as-if-I-had-never sinned, righteous, cleared to be in God's presence, imagine Jesus grabbing your hand and walking into the throne room of GOD and saying this is My brother or My sister.

- **Redeemed;** Imagine a large, _**"Paid in Full stamp"**_. Believers have been redeemed from the curses of the law. No longer are you from Adam and Eve's side of the family but now you have been adopted by GOD Almighty. The cost of your adoption has been **"paid in full"** by Jesus. You have been brought home by Jesus to the Fathers house and Father GOD has adopted you and given you His name. Jesus is your big brother.
- **Sanctified;** Made Holy by Jesus Christ and **set apart** for GOD. The Believers spirit is **made holy** by the elimination of the universe of sin through the payment for all sin and the absorbing of all the wrath of the Father by Jesus Christ. Believers are Saintified.
- **Wisdom** is the proper use of the knowledge of GOD, through communication, relationship, and action with "GOD, the Holy Spirit"; ready to accomplish every good work GOD has for you to do. Remember; **It is the truth you know that sets you free.**

Without a clear understanding of these four gifts, Believers can read your Bible **and not** receive the power of the words spoken by GOD about you. These four words are the centerpiece of the Believers inheritance from the estate of Jesus Christ. If you do not know what they are, you have no idea how to put them to work in your heart and your mind and you will not be able to activate a mindset in your brain for this part of your inheritance in Jesus Christ. Think about; "what these words say to you about your identity" and move up in class to being a child of GOD.

Relationship with Father GOD is not mandatory, but The lack of a relationship comes with a death penalty.
Hard Truth or wake-up call?

In my personal polling, the following questions should be answered in the affirmative but sadly they are not. Very few Christians, when asked the following questions, have a positive answer. The people polled certainly do not have an image relating to their righteousness, sanctification, redemption nor the availability of the Lord's wisdom.

- Do you consider your present life to be the "more abundant life" Christ offered? John 10:10-11 The usual answer is **no.**

- Have you received the Holy Spirit since you believed and is their evidence in your life that the Holy Spirit is inside you? John 14:26 The usual answer **I don't know.**

- Have you accomplished greater works than Jesus did because he has gone to be with the Father and will answer your prayers with yes and amen? (John 14:12-14) The usual answer is **no.**

- Do you know what GOD given authority you have as a Christian? The usual answer is **no.**

- Is the direction of your life concentrated on loving GOD and serving others more significantly than yourself? The usual answer is **I don't know**

but I am trying.
How do you answer these questions?

Where is your relationship
with GOD?

> Galatians 2:20 I have been crucified with Christ. It is no longer I who live, but Christ who lives in me. And the life I now live in the flesh I live by faith of the Son of God, who loved me and gave himself for me.

Spend a few minutes thinking about this scripture and allow the love of your Savior to cover you with an awesome presence of GOD's overwhelming love for you. Your question is, "What kind of relationship do you want?"

If you choose to have an intimate 24/7 relationship with GOD, listen to this promise. Stop and close your eyes and let your imagination see yourself speaking to "GOD, the Holy Spirit" and confirming the goal, you and "GOD, the Holy Spirit" want to accomplish for today. Listen to the Apostle Paul tell you about the Holy Spirit.

> The Holy Spirit will give you the Spirit of wisdom and of revelation in the knowledge of (Jesus) him, having the **eyes of your hearts enlightened,** that you may know what is the hope to which he has called you, **what are the riches of his glorious inheritance in the saints, and what is the immeasurable greatness of his power toward us who believe**. Ephesians 1:17-20

God, the Holy Spirit, 34

Believers need to imagine "our place" in GOD's world, **we are GOD's family,** Jesus called us brothers and sisters. Father GOD called Believers, His children. Believers are destined to Heaven for eternity, we have the freedom of future knowledge and victory over death of the body. We have been given the peace of Jesus Christ for our lives. These blessings are facts and they are not in dispute. **The only question is do you believe you have been given these blessings?** If these promises of GOD **are not** brain mindsets, your mind cannot activate them for the issues of life?

The Lord has given Believers the victory over the enemy, but instead of living" from the victory of Jesus", Believers can find themselves influenced by the enemy and trying to "win a victory" for the Lord. If you fight to win victory for the Lord, you will only be able to summon man-made forces, if you believe _Jesus is the victory that overcomes the world,_ Believers can call on the victory, GOD has won, the Lord's victory is your inheritance and "GOD, the Holy Spirit" is inside you as your executor of the Lord's inheritance.

The Power of the Scripture

When, as a Believer, you feel **fear, Stop and think,** the Lord has **not** given Believers the spirit of fear but the Spirit of love, power, and a sound mind. (2nd Timothy 1:6-7)

Listen to the following verses and put them in your heart and visualize receiving these promises from GOD, like walking across a graduation stage in cap and gown, and GOD giving a diploma that has these verses written inside.

Proverbs 3:5 Trust in the LORD with all thine heart; and lean not unto thine own understanding.
In all thy ways acknowledge him,
and he shall direct thy paths.
Be not wise in thine own eyes:
fear the LORD,
and depart from evil.
It shall be health to thy navel,
and marrow to thy bones.
Honour the LORD with thy substance,
and with the first fruits of all thine increase:
So shall thy barns be filled with plenty,
and thy presses shall burst out
with new wine.
If I were a doctor, this proverb would be a prescription for every patient. Believers, who lean on GOD, relate to GOD, and acknowledge GOD in His perfectness, can be assured of a divine outcome. If Believers can consume ourselves with thanksgiving and acknowledging GOD for his creation and depend on GOD's word for direction; His Spirit will lead us into divine paths. Listen to this Psalm reminding Believers about GOD's love for Believers.

My Refuge and My Fortress
Psalms 91:1 He who dwells in the shelter of the Most High will abide in the shadow of the Almighty.
I will say to the LORD,
"My refuge and my fortress,
my God, in whom I trust."
For he will deliver you
from the snare of the fowler

and from the deadly pestilence.
He will cover you with his pinions,
and under his wings you will find refuge;
his faithfulness is a shield and buckler.
You will **not** fear the terror of the night,
nor the arrow that flies by day,
nor the pestilence that stalks in darkness,
nor the destruction that wastes at noonday.
A thousand may fall at your side,
ten thousand at your right hand,
but it **will not** come near you.
You will only look with your eyes
and see the recompense of the wicked.
Because you have made the LORD
your dwelling place— the Most High, who is my refuge—
no evil shall be allowed to befall you,
no plague come near your tent.
For he will command his angels
concerning you
to guard you in all your ways.
On their hands they will bear you up,
Lest you strike your foot against a stone.
You will tread on the lion and the adder;
the young lion and the serpent
you will trample underfoot.
"Because he holds fast to me
in love,
I will deliver him;
I will protect him,
because he knows my name.

God, the Holy Spirit, 37

When he calls to me,
I will answer him;
I will be with him in trouble;
I will rescue him and honor him with long life
I will satisfy him
and show him my salvation."

Psalms were written before the new Covenant but the subject of the love of GOD for His children has transferred from the old covenant to the presence of "GOD, the Holy Spirit" being inside Believers in the Temple with the Believers born-again Spirit.

> 1st Corinthians 3:16 Do you not know that **you are God's temple and that God's Spirit dwells in you?**

Commitment to GOD and relationship with GOD is the only protection against the storms of life. Everything in life is going great until it isn't. When things are going great, it is important to expand your intimate relationship with "GOD, the Holy Spirit", so that you are prepared when things are not going great. The 91st Psalm talks about Believers using your imagination to see our "GOD as our fortress and our refuge"; it is so important to live in the Kingdom of GOD, imagine yourself in the scripture, "GOD's angels surround you and His Spirit is inside you". Set up mindsets in your brain by consistently meditating on the things of GOD.

These scriptures are to help create images and promote pondering about GOD in the Believers mind to bring Believers closer to an intimate relationship with GOD and

practice building relationship; based on communication, meditation, and creating images of the greatness of your GOD, in your heart, and by exploring the Bible.
Listen as the Apostle Paul talks about the knowledge and power available in a relationship with Jesus Christ and "GOD, the Holy Spirit". Ephesians 1:17-21

That the God of our Lord Jesus Christ,
The Father of glory, **may give you the Spirit of wisdom and of revelation in the knowledge of him,**
having the eyes of your hearts enlightened,
that you may **know (be intimate with)**
what is the hope to which
he has called you,
what are the riches of
his glorious inheritance in the saints,
and what is the immeasurable greatness
of his power
toward us who believe,
according to the working of his great might
that he worked in Christ
when he raised him from the dead and
seated him at his right hand
in the heavenly places,
far above all rule and authority
and power and dominion,
and **above every name**
That is named,
not only in this age
but also in the one to come.

God, the Holy Spirit, 39

And he put all things under his feet
     and gave him as head over all things
          to the church, which is his body,
  the fullness of him who fills all in all.

Remember; mankind is a created being; we are not accidents of nature and we have a destiny implanted in us by GOD Almighty and we have a calling to love our Creator. *The challenge* for Believers is to develop a love for GOD **that approaches the love Jesus Christ and GOD Almighty have for Believers.** A personal relationship based on love for GOD, in concert with "GOD, the Holy Spirit", will lead Believers to inspired results.

> 1st Corinthians 13:4-8 Love is patient and kind; love does not envy or boast; it is not arrogant or rude. It does not insist on its own way; it is not irritable or resentful; It does not rejoice at wrongdoing, but rejoices with the truth. Love bears all things, believes all things, hopes all things, endures all things. Love never ends.

Conclusion: Believers are Spirit beings passing by Earth on our way to Eternity.

Faith worketh by love, or faith works based on how much you believe GOD loves you. GOD does not have love, GOD is love. Can you receive GOD's love, it is abiding inside you right now, can you believe it, will you allow the love of GOD to inspire your daily activities?

The Journey to discover "GOD, the Holy Spirit"

Chapter 2

Jesus died to give Believers "GOD, the Holy Spirit"
To abide with Believers and be "on" and "inside" you.

Jesus was the first comforter and has promised to send "GOD, the Holy Spirit" (the Second Comforter), to Believers; **the second comforter is the Spirit of Jesus Christ inside Believers without His human body,** Listen to Jesus from the discourse at the Last Supper telling the disciples about the sending of "GOD, the Holy Spirit";

> John_14:16 And I will pray the Father, and **he shall give you another Comforter,** that he may abide with you forever;
> John_14:26 But the **Comforter,** which is the Holy Spirit, whom the Father will send in my name, **he shall teach you all things, and bring all things to your remembrance,** whatsoever I have said unto you.
> John_15:26 But when the **Comforter** is come, whom I will send unto you from the Father, even the **Spirit of truth,** which proceeds from the Father, **he shall testify of me:**
> John_16:7 Nevertheless I tell you the truth; It is expedient for you that I go away: for if I go **not away,** the **Comforter will not come** unto you; but if I depart, I will send him unto you.

The New Covenant with "GOD, the Holy Spirit", resident

in Believers, **is the most dynamic era of GOD on Earth,** since the Garden of Eden, before sin. Before the breaking of covenant with GOD, by Adam and Eve, GOD in the fullness of all three aspects of GOD walked and talked to Adam and Eve daily. There was no impediment between mankind and GOD because there was harmony in the earth and Mankind was perfect in all aspects, body, soul, and Spirit. The breaking of covenant by Adam and Eve caused a Spiritual separation of GOD, Mankind, and the Earth. This is the longest sentence in the book, read it several times. GOD's solution to mankind's separation was to make a covenant with Jesus and send Jesus to live the "covenant of the Law" perfectly, to enable GOD to redeem Mankind, through the Lord's death, resurrection, and absorbing all the punishment, for every choice of mankind to live unto themselves instead of living unto GOD, in the world, from the beginning of time until the end of time. Jesus was one man on earth, but when He ascended to Heaven, He sent the Holy Spirit of GOD to seal the salvation of billions of Believers and to be with all of the Believers forever.

Two questions.

> **Do you see** and understand the change in the personification of GOD in the flesh, to the sending of "GOD, the Holy Spirit" to abide inside Believers as a seal to salvation and an anointing through being baptized with "GOD, the Holy Spirit"? Jesus was GOD with Believers, as a human, and now Believers have "GOD, the Holy

Spirit" to be inside Believers, and available "to be on" Believers who ask, creating the most personal of all relationships.

Do you draw from the spiritual world, for your life, in the physical world? **If not,** you are living with man-made plans and results. This does not mean that you can't go to Heaven, but you can't have a meaningful relationship with "GOD the Holy Spirit" on Earth, right now and not live in the spiritual world of faith of Believers and the grace of "GOD, the Holy Spirit". Believers cannot have a relationship without communicating with "GOD, the Holy Spirit" and that requires faith.

Think about GOD abiding inside Believers, inside you, right now!

1st Corinthians 3:16-17 Know ye not that ye are the temple of God, and that the Spirit of God dwelleth in you? If any man defile the temple of God, him shall God destroy; for the temple of God is holy, which temple ye are.

1st Corinthians 6:19-20 What? know ye not that your body is the temple of the Holy Spirit which is in you, which ye have of God, and ye are not your own? For ye are bought with a price: therefore glorify God in your body, and in your spirit, which are God's.

Now let us study in scripture "GOD, the Holy Spirit" being **on and** in Believers.

Luke_11:13 If ye then, being evil, know how to

give good gifts unto your children: how much more shall your heavenly **Father give the Holy Spirit** to them that **ask him?**

Luke 3:16 John, (the Baptist), answered them all, saying, "I baptize you with water, but he (Jesus) who is mightier than I is coming, the strap of whose sandals I am not worthy to untie. **He (Jesus) will baptize you with the Holy Spirit and fire.**

John 1:33 And I knew him not: but he that sent me to baptize with water, the same said unto me, Upon whom thou shalt see the Spirit descending, and remaining on him, **the same is he (Jesus) which baptizeth with the Holy Spirit.**

Many denominations and churches teach; "GOD, the Holy Spirit" is included in the Salvation experience and scripture backs that up, but that teaching is **not the complete truth** and does not include a second anointing from the baptism with "GOD, the Holy Spirit". The teaching of salvation that includes "GOD, the Holy Spirit" as a seal to your salvation can keep the Holy Spirit locked in the Old Covenant concerned with convicting Believers of their works of the flesh. This teaching of the Holy Spirit convicting Believers of sin is not scriptural, it is incomplete, and completely antithetical to Hebrews 8:10-13 and Hebrews 10:13-18. Hebrews 8 and 10 announces **GOD no longer remembers Believers sin. The New Covenant states that GOD remembers the Believers sins no more and is merciful to your iniquities and agrees to be your GOD and Believers to be GOD's people.**

Therefore, there must be another purpose for GOD giving Believers "GOD, the Holy Spirit" as another comforter because GOD does not remember the Believers sin. Convicting **Saints** of their sin is not a scriptural job for the Holy Spirit. "GOD, the Holy Spirit" convicts' **unbelievers** of their sin and convicts Believers of their righteousness. Do not be misled by 1st John 1:9 as forgiveness for Saints for daily sin, because GOD remembers Believer's sin no longer.

This verse (1st John 1:9) is an invitation to the Gnostics for repentance and salvation, not a method of penance for Christians who are committing works of the flesh.

Listen again to the foundational scripture for the beginning of the New Covenant and pay close attention to the five "I will statements from GOD".

> **For this is the Covenant** that I will make with the house of Israel after those days, declares the Lord: **I will put my laws into their minds, and write them on their hearts, and I will be their God,** and they shall be my people. And they shall not teach, each one his neighbor and each one his brother, saying, 'Know the Lord,' for they shall all know me, from the least of them to the greatest. **For I will be merciful toward their iniquities, and I will remember their sins no more."** In speaking of a new covenant, he makes the first one obsolete. **And what is becoming obsolete (Old Covenant) and growing old is ready to vanish away.** Hebrews 8:10-13

Now let us add some logic; If the old covenant is obsolete, and GOD does not remember the Believers sins, and is merciful to your iniquities and Jesus has made the Believer's Spirit perfect: the responsibility of the Holy Spirit **cannot be to convict Believers of sin, because GOD does not remember your sins.** The church thinking that "GOD, the Holy Spirit" is convicting Believers of sins is counterintuitive, because GOD does not remember Believers sins. **To further destroy** the idea that "GOD, the Holy Spirit" is in Believers to convict Believers of sin, listen to Jesus in John 17:23-26 and Colossians 1:27-28.

> John 17:23-26 I in them, and thou in me, **that they may be made perfect in one;** and that the world may know that thou hast sent me, and **hast loved them,** as thou hast loved me. Father, I will that they also, whom thou hast given me, be with me where I am; that they may behold my glory, which thou hast given me: for GOD loves me before the foundation of the world.

Did you see it; Sinners **cannot** be part of Jesus Christ. That is why Jesus made our New Creation Spirit perfect. Here is another confirmation:

> Colossians 1:27-28 To whom God would make known what is the riches of the glory of this mystery among the Gentiles; **which is Christ in you, the hope of glory:** Whom we preach, warning every man, and teaching every man in all wisdom; **that we may present every man perfect in Christ Jesus:**

How can we resolve the conflicting message of the

church and the Biblical operation of "God, the Holy Spirit"? "God, the Holy Spirit" is inside Believers to point out the love GOD has for Believers, so that they will be motivated to live right. **"Living Holy" out of fear is wrong.** GOD desires transformation by the renewing of your mind and a loving relationship with "GOD, the Holy Spirit", not behavior modification for fear GOD will "ZAP" you. Constantly remind yourself that "GOD, the Holy Spirit" is inside you to lead and inspire Believers to your abundant life on Earth. **GOD does not remember the sins he has forgotten.**

Listen to Jesus list what "GOD, the Holy Spirit" will do when He is inside Believers in the following scripture.

> John 16:12 "I (Jesus) still have many things to say to you, but you cannot bear them **now. When the Spirit of truth ("GOD, the Holy Spirit") comes, he will guide you into all the truth,** for he will not speak on his own authority, but **whatever he hears he will speak, and he will declare to you the things that are to come.** He will glorify me, for "GOD, the Holy Spirit" will take what is mine and declare it to you. All that the Father has is mine; **therefore I said that "GOD, the Holy Spirit" will take what is mine and declare it to you.**

Note: Did you see that everything GOD owns, has been given to Jesus Christ and Jesus has given it to GOD, the Holy Spirit for Believers. "GOD, the Holy Spirit" is going to guide you into all truth, declare to you the gifts given (past tense) to you by Jesus Christ, and to tell you things to come.

**Believers have been given the gift of
"GOD, the Holy Spirit"
Open the gift and embrace
the love of Jesus, the Giver.**

A Believer cannot be the "god of your life" when things are going well, and at the first sign of serious adversity, think you can call on the **GOD of the Universe** to rescue you from the ditch. First off, the ditch is the result of man-made plans and always leaves scars. **The destiny of every blood bought Believer is to have a relationship with GOD; that relationship needs to be the first focus in the Believers life and the second focus is to march toward your destiny, acting on the will of GOD, written in your heart, and illuminated through communication with "GOD, the Holy Spirit".** "GOD, the Holy Spirit" will never lead you into a ditch but instead, if GOD is your shepherd, "God, the Holy Spirit" will lead Believers into green valleys, by the still waters, and you shall not lack.

Think about the scriptures below and the promise of GOD's communication with Believers.

Jesus said, "His sheep **hear his voice,** know Him, and **follow Him."** (John 10:27)

John 16:13 When the Spirit of truth comes, he ("GOD, the Holy Spirit") **will guide you** into all the truth, **for he will not speak** on his own authority, but whatever he hears **he will speak,** and **he will declare** to you the **things that are to come.**

Believers **have a right** to have a relationship with GOD Almighty through "GOD, the Holy Spirit" of Jesus Christ. Believers can see and hear from these scriptures that Believers are expected to hear from GOD, to speak to GOD, to know GOD intimately, and follow GOD. Now that Believers can abide in GOD and GOD is abiding in Believers, Believers should speak or act following a confirmation in your heart from "GOD, the Holy Spirit".

The question; Have you spoken to GOD this hour? Have you worshipped GOD today? Are you consulting and conversing with "GOD, the Holy Spirit" 200 times a day? How about 10 times a day or must you admit that you do not speak to GOD or listen to GOD, and possibly you do not know conversations with GOD are possible? Believers can go to church and occasionally read the Bible and go to Heaven but live their life in their own power, devoid of any divine results and always living in the ditch of despair wondering where GOD is, when GOD is inside you wanting a relationship.

Consider this: In the Garden of Eden before sin, Adam and Eve walked and talked to GOD each afternoon, what do you think they talked about? There was no sin, no poverty, no devil, no need for food, clothing, or shelter; what do you imagine the conversations were about?

As a Believer, **who has been made perfect in Jesus Christ, and our physical needs are supplied by Father GOD, and "GOD, the Holy Spirit" is abiding with Believers for comfort and power;** what should our conversations with GOD be about?

The answer is the Believers conversations should be filled

with love, thanksgiving, acknowledgement and praise to GOD, for His world and His love for Believers. If Believers know GOD and let GOD lead their lives, they will never see the ditch of despair, lack, or depression. The Believer's relationship with GOD requires Believers to know GOD, be intimate with GOD, be focused on GOD, and speak and listen to GOD.

> GOD's creations: His world, His word, His love, His Spirit, and His peace are gifts to you the Believer, GOD's love child.

The "Good News for Believers"; when you are involved in a full on, intense relationship with "GOD, the Holy Spirit" you will not be calling GOD to get you out of the ditch of despair. Believers who consult "GOD, the Holy Spirit" **will not** be led into a ditch. Concentrate on this; Jesus only did what He saw the Father do. **And "GOD, the Holy Spirit" is only going to lead you to do what he sees the Father and our Lord do and say.** Therefore, Believers should do and say what we read in the word of GOD and hear from "GOD, the Holy Spirit" and do acts of kindness Jesus did.

Believers not depending on "GOD, the Holy Spirit" are living in the "dark ages".

> 1st Corinthians 2:9-13 But as it is written, eye hath not seen, nor ear heard, neither have entered into the heart of man, the things which God hath prepared for them that love him. **But God hath revealed them unto us by his Spirit:** for the Spirit searches all things, yea, the deep things

of God. For what man knows the things of a man, save the spirit of man which is in him? even so the things of God knows no man, **but the Spirit of God.** Now we (Believers) have received, not the spirit of the world, **but the spirit which is of God; that we might know the things that are freely given to us of God.**

Notice: "GOD, the Holy Spirit" is with your born-again Spirit to point out your right-standing with GOD and to tell you things freely given to Believers by GOD. Your conscience will let you know that you have missed a mark and you can apologize. Believers have not received "the spirit of the world" but **the Spirit of GOD.**

If you **do not know or communicate with "GOD, the Holy Spirit"** Believers **cannot** learn about the things freely given Believers by GOD. Also, it is very important to recognize that the Believers **speak the wisdom** taught the Believer by "GOD, the Holy Spirit" but only if you know and communicate with "GOD, the Holy Spirit".

A simple answer to a complex problem.

The area in your life where Believers are experiencing the most adversity is the place in your life where you need your positive mindsets of the word of GOD giving you GOD's perspective and the power to speak "life" to your situation. Studying, meditating and imagining the promises from the Bible produces "hope" and readies your faith to act. Studying the Bible will renew the Believers mind to your authority as a "child of GOD", and your knowledge of the word of GOD will allow more conversation with "GOD, the Holy Spirit" who speaks to you by faith in GOD's word written in your heart. Think about the 23rd Psalm.

> The Lord is my shepherd and I shall not lack,
> He leadeth me into green pastures,
> GOD leadeth me beside the still waters, He restoreth my Soul,
> GOD leads me into the paths of righteousness, for His namesake.
> Even though I walk through the valley of the shadow of death,
> I will fear no evil, for GOD is with me; your rod and your staff, they comfort me.
> GOD prepares a table before me in the presence of my enemies;
> you anoint my head with oil; my cup overflows.
> Surely goodness and mercy shall follow me all the days of my life,
> and I shall dwell in the house of the LORD forever.

The answer to all of the problems of every Christian and every church body, and every denomination **is a meaningful relationship with "GOD, the Holy Spirit".** GOD can lead you, but it is of no value **if you do not follow.** If there is **no real trust in GOD and His word;** the idea that you are having a relationship with GOD becomes a **wish** or a **hope** and is not a reality. Do you see the difference in faith in GOD or wishing and hoping in GOD? Wishing is fruitless and **Hope is always in the future** and is not active in your life, but **faith is now and is active in**

your life situations, right now. Living life in the power of "GOD the Holy Spirit" is now and operates in faith. Waiting for your spiritual life with GOD <u>until Heaven is a hope</u> and is all in the future and will not be active in your life today.

Make a note; **Jesus did not die for you to have a ticket to heaven, Jesus died to make Believer righteous, so Father GOD and Jesus could give Believers "GOD, the Holy Spirit", to all who would believe on Him and put Jesus on the throne of their life, Heaven is an added blessing.** If Believers do not communicate with "GOD, the Holy Spirit", is there any evidence that you have entered the post-cross, **New Covenant era,** resulting from the Lord's sacrifice. Think about it; Was the Lord's sacrifice in vain?

Any and all thoughts or actions of doubt or unbelief denigrate the sacrifice of Jesus Christ and say that something you say or do is more powerful than the sacrifice of Jesus Christ.

Do not make Earth your home.
Live in relationship with GOD's Spirit.

The benefits to receiving "GOD, the Holy Spirit" is a lifeline to the Spiritual world for the believer. Stop and think about the operation of "GOD, the Holy Spirit" for the Believer.

"GOD, the Holy Spirit" offers:
To comfort the Believers.
John 14:26

God, the Holy Spirit, 53

To teach Believers all things.
John 14:26
To bring all things to your remembrance.
John 14:26
To search the deep things of GOD.
1st Corinthians 2:9-13
To declare the gifts GOD has given Believers.
1st Corinthians 2:9-13
To guide Believers into all things.
John 16:12
To declare to Believers things to come.
John 16:12
To give Believers words of reply when persecuted.
Mark 13:11

Do you see, **Jesus died to send Believers "GOD, the Holy Spirit"** to all who would put Jesus on the "Throne of your life", that is the gospel. Think about it, in every situation in life, if Believers will stop and ask, "God, the Holy Spirit" for information or for confirmation of an action, Believers can hear from "GOD, the Holy Spirit" in your Spirit by faith, right now.

Do you understand the difference between
The New Testament and The New Covenant?

Some churches do not make a great distinction between the **Bible's New testament** and the **New Covenant,** which can cause Christians to live under the law without the power of the New Covenant and "GOD, the Holy Spirit".

Remember; the job of the Holy Spirit is not to convict believers of sin but to convict Believers of the righteousness given at the cross to Believers.

Do you understand there is a difference between the "New Covenant" and the "New Testament"? The New Testament is a division in the Bible separating the time before Jesus and the time during and after Jesus Christ on Earth.

The four Gospels are a picture of Jesus living **under the law** of the old covenant and setting up salvation and the reconciliation of Believers to GOD, **so that Jesus can start the New Covenant by sending "GOD, the Holy Spirit" to Believers.**

Listen to Jesus announce the beginning of the **New Covenant with "GOD, the Holy Spirit";**

Acts 1:8-9 But you will receive power when the Holy Spirit has come upon you, and you will be my witnesses in Jerusalem and in all Judea and Samaria, and to the end of the earth." And when he had said these things, as they were looking on, he was lifted up, and a cloud took him out of their sight.

The New Covenant was delivered to Believers by Jesus Christ after He ascended to Heaven. Acts 1:9 first evidence of the new Church body of Jesus Christ.

Your New Creation Spirit was the fulfillment by Jesus Christ of the Covenant of the Law and the Prophets, this is the beginning of the New Covenant and it starts with the ascension of the

Lord to Heaven. It was announced at the Sermon by Apostle Peter at Pentecost. Salvation and its benefits and the gift of "GOD, the Holy Spirit" are given to Believers and the Church of Jesus Christ was started.

Why is it important to know when the New Covenant started?

The "New Testament" starts at Matthew 1:1, but the New Covenant did not start at the birth of Jesus, or when Jesus was baptized with the Holy Spirit, or when Jesus died; the **"New Covenant"** started **with the Lord's resurrection.** After the Resurrection, Jesus had conquered sin and death to honor His commitment to Father GOD and fulfill his covenant to reconcile mankind to GOD.

It is important **to know when the New Covenant started** because GOD has always dealt with Mankind according to covenants or agreements. **Believers desperately need to know the difference between the covenant Jesus lived under (The Law) and the New Covenant Jesus died to give Born-again Believers.** Listen to this scripture several times to receive its full impact.

Galatians 4:4-7 But when the fullness of time had come, **God sent forth his Son,** born of woman, **born under the law,** to redeem those who were under the law, so **that we might receive adoption as sons.** And because **you are** sons, **God has sent the Spirit of his Son into our hearts,** crying, "Abba! Father!" So you are no longer a slave, but a son, and if a son, then **an heir through God.**

Notice: Jesus was born and **lived under the covenant of the law.** Jesus redeemed Believers from **the curse of the law** and GOD has sent the Spirit of Jesus to be in our hearts **as evidence of the New Covenant. Believers are now an heir of Jesus Christ, not when we die but as of the date of the Lord's death.** Look at this next section to see the difference in the construction of the New Testament after **Jesus sent "GOD, the Holy Spirit".**

The words in the New Testament
give evidence to the timing of the New Covenant.

Let us examine the word and use of **"Grace"** as **part of the evidence of the start of the "New Covenant".** Everyone quotes the scripture that, Believers are saved by grace through faith; **but the word "grace" does not appear in the New Testament until Jesus resurrection** except in two references to Jesus being "grace and truth" in the Gospel of John.

> *Jesus never used the word "Grace", never taught on "grace", because "grace" in Spiritual terms would not be available until the Lord's resurrection.*

Ephesians 2:8 For by grace you have been saved through faith. And this is not your own doing; **it is the gift of God,**

Think about this; GOD is Love; Jesus Christ **is grace** and truth, and **"GOD, the Holy Spirit"** is the Spirit of Jesus

Christ and the Spirit of Truth. The gift of "Grace" could not be given until Jesus reconciled Believers to GOD and Believers were free from the nature of sin and were in right-standing with GOD. The word "Grace" appears 121 times after the Lord's ascension to Heaven and only twice in all the Gospels; announcing that Jesus was grace.

Do you see the importance of the graduation from Jesus, **with us on earth living under the law,** to Jesus reconciling Believers to GOD and giving His Spirit to be "in and on" Believers? **There is an important significance to the fact that "Grace" was not available until Jesus ascended to Heaven and sent "GOD, the Holy Spirit"; this transition is the beginning of the New Covenant.** The Lord's ascension is the connection between the saving grace of Jesus Christ and the New Covenant. Its author, Jesus Christ, and its executor, "GOD, the Holy Spirit".

Listen to the references of Jesus being grace and truth.

> John 1:14-17 And the Word became flesh and dwelt among us, and we have seen his glory, glory as of the only Son from the Father, **full of grace and truth.** (John bore witness about him, and cried out, "This was he of whom I said, 'He who comes after me ranks before me, because he was before me.'") For from his fullness we have all received, **grace upon grace.** For the law was given through Moses; **grace and truth came through Jesus Christ.**

Upon this foundational scripture The Apostle Paul and the other new testament authors use the word "Grace" 121 times to link the unmerited favor of the New Covenant of

GOD to Believers through "GOD, the Holy Spirit". **Now the flesh of Jesus has become Spirit and dwells in Believers, full of grace and truth.**

Another corroboration to the timing of New Covenant is the use of the word "Disciple". Until the Lord ascends into Heaven, the word "Disciples" is used in the New Testament referring to a student of the Master and is used 228 times in the 4 Gospels and Acts and **not one time** after Jesus ascended into Heaven. After the ascension, "GOD, the Holy Spirit" is available to be in the hearts of Believers to teach all things and bring into remembrance everything Jesus has said and to declare to Believers things to come. John 16:12

Churches concentrate on introducing unbelievers to Jesus Christ, as Savior, to forgive the individual sin of living unto themselves, without a Savior, but rarely or never offer an introduction to "GOD, the Holy Spirit" or to lay hands on or give scripture to guide the Believer to receive the baptism in the Holy Spirit. The introduction to Jesus for the forgiveness of sin, **is important,** and is your ticket to Heaven. **The baptism in the Holy Spirit and a relationship with "GOD, the Holy Spirit" is the foundation of the more abundant life in Christ Jesus on Earth and a return of the relationship with Father GOD similar to the relationship of Adam, Eve, and Father GOD in the Garden of Eden before the fall.**

> John_14:26 But the **Comforter,** *which is the Holy Spirit,* whom **the Father** will send **in my name, he shall teach you all things, and bring all things to your remembrance,** whatsoever I have said unto

you.

Notice the timing; Also notice that all three persons of the Godhead are participating. GOD only sends the Holy Spirit to **Believers (after salvation),** and the sending of "GOD, the Holy Spirit" to be "ON" Believers happens after you believe in your need for a Savior, are saved and "GOD, the Holy Spirit" is inside you. Logically there is a second experience with "GOD, the Holy Spirit" confirmed in verse John14:17.

"You know him, for he dwells with you and will be in you".

Continuing the discussion of this personal relationship, GOD desires to have with Believers.

Believers are living in **the New Covenant** which is part of **the New Testament. Part of the mission of Jesus Christ was to fulfill the law and the Prophets, so that His death and receipt of the wrath of GOD for the past, present, and future sin of the world; the "Old Covenant" could be done away with and sin remembered no more.** Think about the timing; Until Jesus sent Believers "GOD, the Holy Spirit" initiating the era of the New Covenant **the world was under the "Old Covenant of the law".**

Why is "GOD, the Holy Spirit"
the next era, with GOD, for believers?

Answer: Our Savior was constrained by His human body; after resurrection Jesus was able to send His Spirit, not constrained by a body, to be in and on all Believers. The big question for Believers is do you TRUST GOD that

"GOD, the Holy Spirit" is inside you and interested in everything you do? Do you believe that GOD wants a personal "love" relationship with you as an individual? Do you want a personal, intimate, intense, 24/7 love relationship with GOD? Listen to the Apostle Paul describe Believers.

> **1st Corinthians 3:16** Do you **not know** that **you are God's temple and that God's Spirit dwells in you?**
>
> 1st Corinthians 6:19 Or do you not know that your body is a temple of the Holy Spirit within you, **whom you have from God? You are not your own, *for you were bought with a price.*** So glorify God in your body.
>
> 1st Thessalonians 4:7 For God has not called us for impurity, but in holiness. Therefore whoever **disregards this, disregards not man but God, who gives his Holy Spirit to you.**

A pre-eminent relationship with GOD cannot be accomplished by two hours on Sunday. Pre-imminent means first or before all.

**GOD made six days of work
and one day of rest for man' body
GOD made Believer's Spirit for a 24/7 relationship.**

It appears; The world and the Church have decided that the Believers relationship with GOD should mirror the construction of the week, GOD's six days of work and one day of rest, but the principle, for the week, was designed for the best maintenance of the physical body not the Spirit of Believers. The relationship with GOD "was and is", always 24 hours a day seven days a week, a pre-eminent focus on GOD. Listen to GOD talking to Joshua about relationship with GOD and His word.

> Joshua 1:8-9 This Book of the Law shall not depart from your mouth, but **you shall meditate on it day and night,** so that you may be careful to do according to all that is written in it. <u>For then you will make your way prosperous, and then you will have good success.</u>

And another word from the Lord.

> Mark 12:30-31 And you shall love the Lord your God **with all your heart and with all your soul and with all your mind and with all your strength.** and 'You shall love your neighbor as yourself'.

Basing your life on GOD first, family and others second, and **you third** is the system that GOD's word declares as the best priority system for life. Now listen to Joshua confirm, to the people of Israel, whom He will follow.

> **Joshua 24:15** And if it is evil in your eyes to serve the LORD, choose this day whom you will serve, whether the gods your fathers served in the region beyond the River, or the gods of the Amorites in whose land you dwell. But as for me and my house, we will serve the LORD."

Listen to Jesus from Matthew 10;

> Matthew 10:37-39 **Whoever loves father or mother more than me is not worthy of me, and**

**whoever loves son or daughter more than me is
not worthy of me. And whoever does not take
his cross and follow me is not worthy of me.**
Whoever finds his life will lose it, and whoever
loses his life **for my sake** will find it.
It is GOD who gives you your children and your life. GOD,
the Father, Jesus Christ, the Redeemer, and "GOD, the
Holy Spirit" are worthy to be praised, worshipped, and
chosen to lead your life every minute of every day. There
is a consequence to choosing anything other than GOD to
follow, serve, and worship. Man-made plans and
leadership will end in man-made outcomes with terrible
consequences.

If GOD is for you, who can be against you?
(Romans 8:31)
The New Covenant for Believers starts with "GOD, the
Holy Spirit" abiding inside Believers for comfort and
power **and to teach Believers how to use the better
promises** Jesus left Believers in His inheritance. "GOD, the
Holy Spirit" of Jesus Christ is available to abide inside you,
have you invited Him inside to fellowship with you? Your
actions, your prayers, and your very thoughts are heard
by GOD inside you, all the time, right now, on Earth.
Believers are never alone and your relationship with
"GOD, the Holy Spirit" is as fresh as the morning dew,
every morning. No Longer do Believers need GOD to act
from Heaven, GOD has given Believers a part of Himself
with resurrection power inside each Believer. In addition,
Jesus has given Believers instructions and **authority** to

act, with standing, as a child of GOD in the Name of Jesus, on earth, right now.

In the New Covenant, Believers have inherited GOD's "I wills" in Hebrews 8 and 10 let us go over them; GOD speaking;

> Hebrews 8:8-12 **I will** make a new covenant with the house of Israel and with the house of Judah (gentiles): For this is the covenant that **I will** make with the house of Israel after those days, saith the Lord; **I will put my laws into their mind, and write them in their hearts:** and **I will** be to them a God, and they shall be to me a people: For **I will** be merciful to their unrighteousness, and **their sins and their iniquities will I remember no more.**

> Hebrews 10:16 This is the covenant that **I will** make with them after those days, saith the Lord, **I will** put my laws into their hearts, and in their minds **will I** write them;

> Hebrews 13:5 Let your conversation be without covetousness; and be content with such things as ye have: for he hath said, **I will never leave thee, nor forsake thee.**

The new paradigm of "GOD, the Holy Spirit" abiding with the Believer, completely changes the old covenant of the law and starts **the New Covenant** through your inheritance from Jesus Christ, Father GOD, and "GOD, the Holy Spirit". **Almighty GOD, Jehovah, El Shaddai, has made an unbreakable Covenant with Believers to honor GOD's I will statements because of what Jesus has done.**

The Covenant cannot be broken because the Believer is not part of the responsibilities of the covenant Believers are just the recipients of the Covenant.

Remember, your individual perception of your relationship with "GOD, the Holy Spirit" will determine the provision from GOD for your endeavors. Where is your level of TRUST in GOD and do you **know;** "what Jesus has reserved for Believers", that you have not even imagined? If you are **not** communicating with "GOD, the Holy Spirit" many times each day; "GOD, the Holy Spirit" cannot tell you things to come, or declare gifts GOD has given you, or teach you about the great things of GOD. **GOD will not force Himself on Believers. It is the Believers responsibility to ask, seek, and knock to enter the Kingdom of GOD.**

Jesus Christ fulfilled the Law and the Prophets.
Performance based religion has changed to
A personal relationship with "GOD, the Holy Spirit".

GOD and Jesus have stored up finished promises for believers to draw from and each promise used by Believers **will partake of the divine nature of GOD.** Listen to this next verse.

> 2nd Peter 1:3 His divine power has granted to us (Believers) **all things** that pertain to life and godliness, **through the knowledge of him** who called us to his own glory and excellence, by which he has granted to us his precious and **very great promises,** so that through them **you may**

become partakers of the divine nature, having escaped from the corruption that is in the world because of sinful desire.

Note: The Believers **who have <u>knowledge</u> of <u>Father GOD and Jesus Christ</u> are granted access to use the promises,** Jesus has reserved for Believers. All things pertaining to life and Godliness are granted to Believers "who believe, speak, and act". To bring **The New Covenant** to life in the Lord's body, the Church; Jesus sent "GOD, the Holy Spirit" and changed the Christians life forever.

Question.
Is "GOD, the Holy Spirit"
a truth and GOD, you do not know?

Do you practice relating to "GOD, the Holy Spirit", Jesus Christ, the Redeemer, and Father GOD, all the time. Do you say a thank you for every flower you see, for the beauty of the sea or the snow-capped mountains, for the sunshine and for the rain, for your salvation, your wonderful body, for the things you have, and for the wisdom to follow "GOD, the Holy Spirit".

What is the level of intimacy in your relationship with "GOD, the Holy Spirit"?

- How will you or how did you welcome "GOD, the Holy Spirit" into the Temple of GOD inside you? 1st Corinthians 3:16
- Knowing that the Holy Spirit is inside you; is your prayer life a conversation or a monologue? John 14:26
- Do you meet every morning with "GOD, the Holy

Spirit" to develop a plan for your day? John 16:13

- Do you pause when you are about to meet someone to hear if "GOD, the Holy Spirit" has a word of knowledge for your meeting? 1st Corinthians 14:1
- Does knowing that "GOD, the Holy Spirit", is inside you, affect your thought life and actions every minute of every day? 1st Corinthians 2:13
- What is "GOD the Holy Spirit's" communication style with you? 1st Corinthians 2:9-13
- Has "GOD, the Holy Spirit" shared with you, an event happening later today, and are you available to listen and act? John 16:12

These questions are not to disparage anyone, but to motivate Believers who are not actively speaking to and listening to the voice of "GOD, the Holy Spirit". Believers can stay out of the ditch of despair and complete more of the works GOD wants to do through Believers, when acting out of a plan born from intimacy with "GOD, the Holy Spirit".

Believers need to practice relating to "GOD, the Holy Spirit" and the Spiritual world because your relationship with GOD will change your earthly domain. Believers have a recognized presence of Almighty GOD inside you. Start living in the Spiritual world with little things like; declaring peace to anxiety or taking the blame at your home for something you did not do. Bring peace to your home and look for the next act of kindness and start with your family. "GOD, the Holy Spirit" is your friend that is more loyal than a brother.

God, the Holy Spirit, 67

Think of receiving "GOD, the Holy Spirit", like getting a new pre-paid credit card, Believers now have to call the sender to activate the card. The most important action as a Believer; you must activate your relationship with "GOD, the Holy Spirit" by thanking GOD and starting to speak to, listen to, follow, and build a relationship with "GOD, the Holy Spirit".

Prayer brings the Believer into fellowship with GOD.
Praise of GOD brings GOD into the Believers presence.
Worship of GOD enlarges the Believers relationship with GOD.

The Journey to discover "GOD, the Holy Spirit"

Chapter 3

**How do I hear with my Spirit, the words,
"GOD, the Holy Spirit" is trying to declare to me?**

How do Believers get started communicating with GOD?
Philemon 1:6 **That the communication of thy faith** may become effectual by the acknowledging of every good thing which is in you in Christ Jesus. Think about what the Apostle Paul is saying, acknowledge every good thing that is inside Believers from the abiding of the Holy Spirit of Jesus Christ. The communication of Believers love for GOD makes the Believers faith effectual. **Notice:** Every good thing inside Believers in Christ Jesus is outside time, invisible, and part of the Spiritual world. The New Covenant brings GOD inside Believers and sets up Believers to act in concert with "GOD, the Holy Spirit" to reign in life through GOD-centered action. "GOD, the Holy Spirit" is in your life to declare the words Jesus gave to Believers for action.

Logic says that memorizing scripture that confirms the promises of Jesus for His heirs is the place to start. Knowing GOD's word gives Believers assurance by faith to words Jesus has authored in the Bible. In communication from Spirit to Spirit knowing what is inside Believers from your love for GOD, Jesus Christ, and "GOD, the Holy Spirit" will illuminate any contradiction, from the enemy, to the promises of GOD in His word so Believers can object and stand on GOD's word.

Jesus had all authority in Heaven and Earth restored at the Cross and has restored Believers authority on earth when Father GOD dethroned the devil. Now Believers with "GOD, the Holy Spirit" must step up and use the authority given to enforce, "who Believers are" in Christ Jesus and follow the destiny you have been given to bring glory to GOD.

Father God's instruction to Adam was to keep the garden and in the New Covenant the Believer is to keep the garden of our hearts and to grow the Kingdom of GOD.

Listen, again, to the words of the New Testament and realize that the following phrases are words of direction for Believers and they **require action** from the Believer not from GOD. Remember the New Covenant is the Believer and "GOD, the Holy Spirit" together on earth as a team. Many Christians have been living without a shepherd praying to get GOD to do something about their man-made plans gone awry. Jesus is "finished" and has sent "GOD, the Holy Spirit" with comfort and power to support the actions of the Believer who will follow divine plans given Believers through "GOD, the Holy Spirit". Believers need to learn the language of "God, the Holy Spirit". **Read through this list of abbreviated scriptures of the language "GOD, the Holy Spirit"** will speak to your Spirit and actions for the Believer to do to restore GOD's will on earth. The language of the Holy Spirit will give you power over a contradiction to GOD's word when confronted in a life issue.

GOD's Spiritual laws and promises are
The language of "GOD, the Holy Spirit"

"Ask, seek, and knock and you shall find
    and it shall be opened" Matthew 7:7
"Cast out devils", Matthew 10:8
"Raise the dead", Matthew 10:8
"Speak to that mountain and cast it into the sea",
    Matthew 21:21
"Love GOD with all your heart", mind, soul and strength
    and your neighbor as yourself" Mark 12:30
"Lay hands on the sick and they shall recover",
    Mark 16:18
"Have faith in GOD" Mark 11:22
"Have faith and not doubt that
    what you say will come to pass", Mark 11:23
"These signs shall follow those who believe",
    Mark 16:17
"Love your neighbor as yourself", Luke 10:27
"Do this in remembrance of Me" Luke 22:19
"Believe on Him, whom He hath sent", John 6:29
"Let not your heart be troubled,
    neither let it be afraid", John 14:1,27
"My peace, I give to you" John 14:27
"Present your bodies as a living sacrifice",
    Romans 12:1-2
"Do not repay evil with evil", Romans 12:21
"Take every thought captive", 2nd Corinthians 10:5

"Abound to every good work", 2nd Corinthians 9:8
"Christ redeemed us from the curse of the law"
    Galatians 3:13
"In Christ you are sons of GOD by faith" Galatians 3:26
"Let no corrupt communication come from
   Your mouth, but lift up others with words"
    Ephesians 4:29
"Giving thanks always for all things unto God",
    Ephesians 5:20
"Be strong in the Lord and the power of His might",
    Ephesians 6:10
"Put on the whole armor of GOD", Ephesians 6:13
"Be angry and not sin", Ephesians 4:26
"Put on your new self", Ephesians 4:24
"Be kind one to another", Ephesians 4:32
"Forgive one another as Christ has forgiven you",
"Be found in Him", Philippians 3:9
"Be anxious for nothing and in everything give thanks",
    Philippians 4:6
"Think on these things, whatsoever are true, excellent, of
    good report, worthy of praise", Philippians 4:8
"In Him are the treasures of wisdom and knowledge"
    Colossians 2:3
"Put off your old self", Colossians 3:9
"Do everything in word or deed,
    do all in the name of Jesus", Colossians 3:17
"Pray unceasingly", 1st Thessalonians 5:17
"Fulfill every resolve for good and every
    work of faith by his power",
    2nd Thessalonians 1:11

God, the Holy Spirit, 72

"Resist the enemy and he will flee", James 4:7
"Anoint with oil and the prayer
          for healing will save the sick", James 5:8
"Be sober minded", 1st Peter 1:13
"Cast your care on Jesus, for He cares for you",
          1st Peter 5:7
"Don't love money, be content with what you have,
          for Jesus will never leave you or forsake you"
          Hebrews 13:5
"Offer the sacrifice of praise, continually" Hebrews 13:15
"Walk in the light as He is in the light"   1st John 1:7
"Prosper and be in health as your soul prospers "
          3rd John 1:2
"Build yourself up on your most holy faith,
          praying in the Holy Spirit" Jude 1:20

These promises of GOD are Spiritual Truths and **Believers have standing or authority to enforce GOD's word when confronted with contradictions to GOD's word.** Listen to the Believers authority given by Jesus before He went to the cross and the report of the 72 followers who were sent out.

> **Matthew 10:1** And he called to him his twelve disciples and gave them authority over unclean spirits, to cast them out, and to heal every disease and every affliction.
>
> **The Return of the Seventy-Two**
> **Luke 10:17** **The seventy-two returned** with joy, saying, "Lord, even the demons are subject to us in your name!" And Jesus said to them, "I saw

Satan fall like lightning from heaven. **Behold, I have given you authority to tread on serpents and scorpions, and over all the power of the enemy, and nothing shall hurt you.** Nevertheless, do not rejoice in this, that the spirits are subject to you, **but rejoice that your names are written in heaven."**

Notice; this is not the Disciples but the return of the seventy two.

<u>Question?</u> How many of the scriptural phrases above could have been an answer to a prayer you called out to GOD for, this year that you did not receive an answer. These phrases are the language of "GOD, the Holy Spirit" used to speak to and guide Believers into green pastures and beside the still water. GOD cares for you more than you know and has given Believers authority and standing to move mountains on Earth using GOD's language in concert with "GOD, the Holy Spirit".

Again Notice: <u>These phrases call for action from the Believer, not from God. Believers have authority on earth.</u>

In the New Covenant, the Believer should **speak to the problem in your life or path about the GOD in your life** and not speak to GOD Almighty about your problem, GOD is finished with His work. Remember, actions born out of your intimate relationship with "GOD, the Holy Spirit" that combine grace and faith **produce divine outcomes.**

When Believers see or are confronted by a contradiction to GOD's word the Believer has the authority to enforce

GOD's word by speaking the truth to the contradiction. Believers have a Born-again Spirit and "GOD, the Holy Spirit" in a temple inside their bodies.

Believers are **not** destined to suffer until we get to Heaven, that idea is just not scriptural. Listen to this scripture from Peter.

> **2nd Peter 1:3-4** His divine power has granted **to us all things that pertain to life and Godliness**, through the knowledge of him who called us to his own glory and excellence, by which he has granted to us his precious and very great promises, so that through them you may become partakers of the divine nature, having escaped from the corruption that is in the world because of sinful desire.

What could be divine about sufferings Jesus died to redeem Believers from?
> **Wrong thinking will lead to wrong living**
> **and Right believing will lead to right living.**

The first step for Believers' relationship building with "GOD, the Holy Spirit" is to lean **not** on your own understanding but to depend on the word of GOD and the Holy Spirit for leadership. This means; stop and consult "GOD, the Holy Spirit" at every contradiction to GOD's word. Believers must stay focused on the goal of doing everything in word and deed, all in the Name of Jesus. To Speak and act all in the Name of Jesus Christ, Believers must be led by "GOD, the Holy Spirit". Listen to the next scripture declaring, what GOD's word accomplishes if you are a Believer and your thought life is based on love.

Psalms 107:20 **He sent out his word and healed them and delivered them from their destruction.** Let them **thank the LORD for his steadfast love,** for his wondrous works to the children of man!

Believers are now filled with "GOD, the Holy Spirit" and Believers are the agents GOD uses, to send out his word to heal, deliver, bless, and testify of GOD's goodness to influence the unbeliever, to want to be a Christian. **The Church body are the arms, legs, and bank of GOD to distribute acts of kindness, gifts of substance, and miracles sanctioned by "GOD, the Holy Spirit" as acts of kindness and as a witness of Jesus Christ and His love.**

**Are you communicating
with "GOD, the Holy Spirit"?**

Remember; the entire chapter of John 10 is Jesus telling Believers about GOD speaking to Believers and leading them in everything they do.

John 10:27 My sheep **hear my voice,** and I know them, and **they follow me.** I give them eternal life, and **they will never perish,** and no one will snatch them out of my hand.

Notice: You are in the Lord's hand and no one can get you out, Jesus is saying that Believers hear His voice, know Him intimately, and they follow Him. **Question,** do you hear "GOD, the Holy Spirit" speaking to you? If the answer is no, we have some work to do,

Let us detour a minute to examine prayer before Jesus

went to the cross and after Jesus made the gift of "GOD, the Holy Spirit" available to Believers. Think about these scriptures about prayer.

Matthew 6:7-8 "And when you pray, do not heap up empty phrases as the Gentiles do, for they think that they will be heard for their many words. Do not be like them, **for your Father knows what you need before you ask him.**

Philippians 4:19 And my **God will supply every need of yours** according to his riches in glory in Christ Jesus. (Context for a giving Believer)

James 4:3 You ask and do not receive, because you ask wrongly, to spend it on your passions.

Mark 7:13 (you are) **Making the word of God of none effect through your tradition,** which ye have delivered: and many such like things do ye.

Question: If GOD knows what you have need of for today, why do we pray for our needs? Even before Jesus went to the cross, He said; Seek first the Kingdom of GOD and all the needs of the world will be supplied to you. Now that Jesus has given believers "GOD, the Holy Spirit" to abide with Believers forever, our prayer life needs to change.

- Do you pray to GOD in Heaven and bypass the fact that "GOD, the Holy Spirit" is living inside you? Or do you believe you have "GOD, the Holy Spirit" inside you?
- Is "GOD, the Holy Spirit" hoping someday to have a conversation with you?
- Have you forgotten that Jesus said, "He was finished" and that he would send Believers "GOD,

the Holy Spirit" to everyone that ask?

- Do you realize, that if you have "GOD, the Holy Spirit" inside you, you have all three persons of the GODHEAD inside your body, because we serve one GOD in three personifications?
- Do you trust GOD enough, to believe that "GOD, the Holy Spirit" is inside you?
- Do you know that Mankind only uses a fraction of the brains capacity and Believers have been given the mind of Christ; will you allow GOD to expand the function of your mind to control the functions of your body and world for your benefit and the benefit of others?
- Is your request to GOD for wisdom purposed with compassion to do acts of kindness in concert with "GOD, the Holy Spirit" inside you?
- Do you only default to GOD when you are in the ditch from personal bad choices?

Now, let us look at the language of prayer from understanding that Believers have "GOD, the Holy Spirit" inside them and Believers have been given authority to act on the promises of GOD. Believers are constantly calling on GOD to get them out of a ditch; **If "GOD, the Holy Spirit" had been consulted, GOD would have led Believers in a different direction to avoid the situation or ditch.** Additionally, many Believers cry out to GOD in Heaven for some request, that the Lord has authorized the petitioner to act on in the power of "GOD, the Holy Spirit" and the Name of Jesus. Look at this next section and take some time to think about prayer before Jesus came to earth, and during Jesus time on earth, and after Jesus sent "GOD, the Holy Spirit".

Jesus is our example and
He spoke to situations in contradiction
to GOD's will and they changed.

Let us investigate prayer with some logic. If you were to pray for prosperity to bless others, what would an answer to that prayer look like?

- GOD **does not** give you wealth, GOD gives you the power to get wealth. If you are praying for a financial need, you must pray and expect men and women to come forth with additional business or gifts of some kind. GOD is not going to make a deposit in your bank account.
- GOD **will not** answer a prayer for something that GOD has given you the authority to accomplish yourself.

   For example:
   Let not your heart be troubled, **neither let it** be afraid.
   Be angry and **sin not.**
   GOD knows what you have need of today and has said seek ye first the Kingdom of GOD and his righteousness and all these needs shall be supplied.

- GOD will not answer a prayer for healing if a miracle is needed.

   If a man was born without a retina in his eye or without a foot, he does not need a healing he needs a reconstructive miracle.

- GOD's grace eliminated the sin-nature from Believers but does not often mitigate the consequences of man-made plans gone awry.

    For example, Moses **killed a man** and was not allowed to enter the promised land.

    King David **committed adultery and killed a man** and was not allowed to build GOD's Temple, the child from adultery died, and most of David's children killed each other over the throne except for Solomon.

    Abraham **committed adultery** with Hagar and the child's descendants grew up to be a thorn in the descendants of Israel, the son of promise, to this day.

- Apostle Paul tells Believers to be happy with what you have and thank God for everything.

Additional ideas that are part of attitude of prayer and relationship with "GOD, the Holy Spirit".

- The lusts of the world come with drama and elements of physical pleasure but are empty and the next day, you must start over without residual joy.
- The happiness of GOD's kingdom comes **without drama and sorrow** and with lasting joy from being redeemed, with liberty from a pure

conscience, and there is plenty of physical pleasure.

- The word from the Apostle Paul is clear; **Present our purpose in life as a living sacrifice as worship for GOD's purpose for our lives, on earth. (Romans 12:1-2) The definition for "worship" is love expressed in words and actions.**

As you love your Creator, renew your mind, and fill your brain with the knowledge of your GOD; your faith in GOD will grow and you will experience the good, acceptable, and the perfect will of GOD. GOD wants Believers to be prosperous to be a blessing to those in need; Believers are stewards of GOD's abundance and received the love of Jesus Christ for distribution to the world, including our own families.

The Apostle Paul is **not telling** Believers to become missionaries. The scripture is saying that by the renewal of your mind to the things of GOD and the giving of your "being" to the service of GOD, **in your vocation and your free time,** will determine whether Believers are able to fulfill the level one, level two, or the top level of GOD's will on earth. And GOD's will for the earth and all of mankind is good.

Planning your day with GOD.

Generally, GOD's plan for Believers will be centered around being a witness of your Lord to your surroundings and on **"being all you can be"** in your family, vocation, and for the benefit of others. When you **do not** make time to meet with GOD, you will not receive the love you need to give away for your day. GOD is love and love is expressed and acted on in the Believer when we consider others more significantly than our selves. If a Believer starts your day without consulting "GOD the Holy Spirit", to plan your day, you will not know what GOD wants you to do and you can't be guaranteed of the supply for your actions today.

Having a plan for your day blessed by "GOD, the Holy Spirit" will dominate doubt during your day. Doubt is constructed of lies from the enemy, from your senses, or from ignorance. **Doubt is not the truth** and is in opposition to the word of GOD and your identity as a child of GOD, a son, and heir to the estate of Jesus Christ. Believers must know the Bible to recognize the lies of the devil. When doubt becomes a stronghold in your brain, your mind must override the stronghold in your brain with the bombardment of the truth of GOD's word. Occasionally, prayer and fasting are needed to destroy strongholds of doubt and error in your brain. Remember there are 10,080 minutes in a week, how many of those minutes are you focusing on GOD and resting in the good plans, GOD has for you, and how many minutes are you depending on your own plan. Listen to GOD's plans in Jeremiah.

> Jeremiah 29:11 **For I know the plans I have for you,** declares the LORD, plans for welfare and not for evil, to give you a future and a hope. Then you will call upon me and come and pray to me, and I will hear you. You will seek me and find me,

when you seek me with all your heart.

This is an Old Testament promise and you no longer have to reach out to heaven to find GOD because GOD is inside you, but the same GOD, has plans for your welfare, and GOD will share those plans, if you will ask. Remember "GOD, the Holy Spirit"' is a Spirit and communicates with Believer's Spirit by faith through your mind and acted on by your voice. Believers, who seek GOD with all your heart and *spend time creating images of the great miracles and admonitions of the Bible will build their faith in GOD and want to know the good plans GOD has for you. The abundant life Jesus has given the Believer must be guarded. Believers must stand against the lies of the enemy, always discerning the spirit of evil seeding thoughts of chaos in your brain.*

Confronting the Contradiction to GOD's word.

The abundant life is knowing and being certain, "who causes problems in life and who created the world and sustains the Believers in their abundant life"? Listen to this scripture but remember that this **scripture was said before Jesus went to the cross** and destroyed the devil's power.

> John 10:10 The thief comes only to steal and to kill and to destroy. I **(Jesus) came** that they may have life and have it abundantly.

The abundant life must be believed and acted upon and protected with control of your thought life. The abundant life is yours, but Believers can live **below** the abundant life when they believe the lies or influence of the thief instead of the abundant life with "GOD, the Holy Spirit".

What is your motivation to be a Christian, a person, a parent, a success, a minister, a choir member? Your motive means everything to GOD. The Believer must give of himself or herself to their relationship with GOD to maintain a pre-eminent relationship with GOD for who GOD is and not for what GOD can do for the Believer. If your relationship with GOD is pre-eminent you will receive what GOD has already stored up for the blessings of Believers. Relationship with GOD and His blessings is like swimming, when you enter the water you get the wet without trying. Think about this, Jesus lived in all the power given mankind, by loving GOD with all His heart, mind, soul, and strength and loving His neighbors as Himself. Living and loving GOD with the totally committed, loving, caring life for the benefit of others allowed the power of a perfect life to operate in faith with miracles galore.

This next chapter is a study of relationship with GOD and how sin affected the Patriarchs of the Bible, relationship with GOD.

The Journey to discover "GOD, the Holy Spirit".

Chapter 4

**Loving GOD with all
your heart, mind, soul, and strength,
Is more important than keeping
the Ten Commandments.**

What is the difference between actions contrary to the Ten Commandments and the sin that will send you to hell? Listen as Jesus details that living unto yourself, without a Savior, is the sin unto death.

2nd Corinthians 5:14-15 **For the love of Christ controls us,** because we have concluded this: **that one has died for all,** therefore all have died; and Jesus died for all, that those who live might **no longer live for themselves** but **for Jesus** who for their sake died and was raised.

2nd Corinthians 5:21 For our sake GOD made Jesus to be sin who knew no sin, so that **in Jesus Believers might become the righteousness of God.**

Colossians 2:13 And you, who were dead in your trespasses and the uncircumcision of your flesh, **God made alive together with Jesus,** having **forgiven us all our trespasses,** by canceling the record of debt that stood against us with its legal demands. This GOD set aside, **nailing it to the cross.**

1st Corinthians 6:19-20 Have you not known that your body is a sanctuary of the Holy Spirit in you, which ye have from God? and **you are not your own,** <u>for you were bought with a price</u>; **glorify, then, God in your body and in your spirit, which are God's.**

If you have experienced GOD's grace, which is Jesus Christ, and if you have chosen to put Jesus Christ on the "Throne" of your life and live unto the LORD, you are saved. **If you, as a Believer, are still living unto yourself and caught up in works of the flesh,** you need to repent or change your mind and focus on the gift of GOD's Son and the fulness of your redemption and your identity in Jesus Christ as Savior.

<u>Notice:</u> Seeking man-made plans and receiving man-made results is living unto yourself and not living unto Jesus Christ who gave Himself for Believers. GOD owns the world and everything in it. Psalm 24 and 50 and Leviticus 27:30 Believers are not our own, for we have been bought with a very high price.

Jesus Christ, your brother, sacrificed Himself to make your Spirit perfect; acceptable in righteousness to receive a part of the Godhead, to live inside you with your Born-again Spirit. The Believers relationship with "GOD, the Holy Spirit" will be measured by your communication with "GOD, the Holy Spirit". What does your communication with GOD resemble, are you communicating moment by moment or seldom to occasional communication and then only in times of dire need?

A beginning question about sin; how can **King David** commit murder and adultery and his love for GOD be counted to David for righteousness? How can **Moses** kill an Egyptian out of anger and his love for GOD be counted as righteousness and how can **Abraham** commit adultery and lie several times and his love for GOD be counted as righteousness?

Is it more important to love GOD with all your heart than to obey the Ten Commandments? How does lawless behavior affect Believers relationship with GOD?

Are Believers to deduce that love and devotion to God is more important than the need to keep the law? The answer is yes, **the Ten Commandments were created to identify the individuals need for a Savior GOD on the throne of each Believer's life.** Wait a minute; **Are not Believers to be holy as Jesus was holy?** The answer is "yes", when motivated by love for GOD and **"no", when motivated by fear and/or condemnation.**

The word "Holy" is not Believers living under the Ten Commandments but is Believers living separated and dedicated to GOD.

Any part of your life not "holy" or "set apart for GOD" will default into man-made decisions and yield man-made outcomes.

Love is more powerful than sin.

The Old Testament patrons, David, Abraham, and Moses found right standing with GOD through their commitment and love for GOD and the Patriarchs were not out of relationship with GOD Almighty because of their works of the flesh. Each of the men suffered loss for their works of the flesh, but the consequences for their iniquity did not cancel their committed relationship with GOD. The Patriarchs were never out of covenant with GOD. **How can this be, what about their sin?**

The Church teaches, "Jesus came to earth full of grace and truth" to fulfill the law so Jesus would qualify to die for the sin of the world, but the **Biblical picture** is that Jesus came to honor his covenant with Father GOD to reconcile mankind to GOD by fulfilling the law and the prophets and receiving the punishment for the sin of all mankind, from the beginning of time until the end of time. The New Covenant gives right standing to Believers therefore, Father GOD could have a relationship with every Believer who chooses Jesus Christ as savior through "GOD, the Holy Spirit" inside Believers.

> The sin of the world **is not** breaking the Ten Commandments but is **having more than the one true GOD in your life.**

Living a set of laws and Church principles does not qualify for holiness. Being holy means to be separated (dedicated) to GOD. Right living needs to be a by-product of loving GOD with all your heart, mind, soul, and strength and loving your neighbor as yourself. Holiness cannot be accomplished by behavior modification; **everyone needs a Savior** and this relationship with GOD must be **the pre-eminent relationship in a Believer's life.**

The act of Jesus reconciling Believers to GOD, allows Father GOD, through the gift of "GOD, the Holy Spirit", to have a personal relationship with each Believer and to speak to and listen to each new child of GOD. Jesus did not come to earth, to die, so that Believers go to heaven, Jesus died to reconcile Believers to himself and Father GOD and give Believers "GOD, the Holy Spirit". Heaven comes with eternal life. Heaven is not as important as eternal life with GOD Almighty. Eternal life starts at salvation. Heaven is in the future.

Foundational Question and Truth.

Do you understand the word sin and the difference between sin and sinning as used in the Bible? The idea of sin and sinning put forth in the Bible is a difficult concept to understand because sin "the noun" is used to represent the sin nature of mankind and identifies the nature of "who" is on the throne of a person's life: GOD or self. If a person has the sin nature on the throne of their life, that person is a sinner by nature. A Believer, who has installed Jesus Christ on the throne of their life, is saved and **cannot be a sinner** because they are justified, sanctified, and redeemed. *Believers are Saints.* Let us look at the complexity of sin when there is no longer any law. The actions of sinning or the word sin used as "a verb"; is either the fruit of a "sin nature" for the unbeliever or if the person has installed Jesus Christ on the throne of their life the action is lawlessness. **Jesus fulfilled the law and where there is no law there is no sin.**

> **Romans 4:15** For the law brings wrath, but **where there is no law there is no transgression.**
>
> **Romans 5:13** for sin indeed was in the world

before the law was given, **but sin is not counted where there is no law.**

The deciding factor to determine sin as the old sin nature or the verb sinning as an evil deed **is the motivation in the heart** of the actor.

>An evil action from a Believer with Jesus Christ installed on the throne of the Believers life is a work of the flesh and will result in severe consequences or results but does not affect GOD's love relationship with you. The Believers Spirit is perfect, being made perfect by the performance of Jesus Christ. No matter what you have done or will do; does not change what **Jesus Christ has done.**

The evil deed done by an <u>un</u>believer with the selfish sin nature on the throne of their life **is sin and will result in death.** The sin nature must be thrown off the throne of the <u>un</u>believer's life, and Jesus Christ enthroned to be saved.

In Romans 6 the word sin is used 14 times as a noun and one time as a verb.

Let us read Romans 6 and study the use of sin as a noun and the one time "sin" is used as a verb. To emphasize the use of sin as a "noun", sin has been changed to **the sin-nature.** It is the rejection of Jesus Christ and the idolatry to self that is the "sin-nature" and that is the sin unto death.

Let us read Romans 6 to understand more:

>**Dead to Sin, Alive to God**
>**Romans 6:1** What shall we say then? Are we to

continue in the sin-nature that grace may abound? Rom 6:2 By no means! How can we **who died to the sin-nature** still live in the sin-nature? Rom 6:3 Do you not know that all of us who have been baptized into Christ Jesus were baptized into his death to eliminate the sin-nature? Rom 6:4 We were buried therefore with him by baptism into death, in order that, just as Christ was raised from the dead by **the glory of the Father,** we too might walk in newness of life. Rom 6:5 For if we have been united with Jesus in a death like his, we shall certainly be united with Jesus in a resurrection like his.

Romans 6:6 We know that our old self (sin-nature) was crucified with Jesus in order that the body of sin-nature might be brought to nothing, so that we would no longer be enslaved to **the sin-nature**. Romans 6:7 For one who has died to the sin-nature **has been set free from the sin-nature** to live for the Savior Jesus Christ. Romans 6:8 **Now if we have died with Christ,** we believe that we will also live with Jesus (on the throne of the Believer's lives). Romans 6:9 We know that Christ, being raised from the dead, will never die again; death no longer has dominion over him. Romans 6:10 For the death Jesus died he died to those with a sin-nature, **once for all, but the life he lives he lives to God.** Romans 6:11 So you also must consider yourselves dead to the sin-nature and alive to God in Christ Jesus (for the throne of your life). Romans 6:12 Let not the sin-nature therefore reign in your mortal body, to make you obey its passions.

The New Covenant life.

Romans 6:13 Do not present your members to the sin-nature as instruments for unrighteousness, but present yourselves to God as those who have been brought from death to life, and your members to God as instruments for righteousness. Romans 6:14 For the sin-nature will **have no dominion** over you, since you (Believers) are not under law but under grace.

Slaves to Righteousness
or slave to yourself?

Romans 6:15 What then? Are we to sin **(verb; acts of evil)** because we are not under law but under grace? By no means! Romans 6:16 Do you not know that if you present yourselves to anyone as obedient slaves, you are slaves of the one whom you obey, either of **the sin-nature,** which leads to death, or of obedience to Christ (on the throne of your life), which leads to righteousness? Romans 6:17 But thanks be to God, that you who were once slaves of **the sin-nature** have become obedient from the heart to the standard of teaching to which you were committed, Romans 6:18 and, having been set free from **the sin-nature,** have become slaves of

God, the Holy Spirit, 92

righteousness of Jesus Christ **(on the throne of your life)**. Romans 6:19 I am speaking in human terms, because of your natural limitations. For just as you once presented your members as slaves to impurity and to lawlessness leading to more lawlessness, **so now present your members as slaves to righteousness leading to sanctification.**

Romans 6:20-21 For when you were slaves of the sin-nature, you were free in regard to righteousness. But what fruit (consequences) were you getting at that time from the things of which you are now ashamed? For the end of those things is death. Romans 6:22 But now that you have been set free from **the sin-nature** and have become slaves of God, **the fruit you get leads** to sanctification and its end, eternal life. Romans 6:23 For the wages of **sin-nature** is death, but **the free gift of God is eternal life in Christ Jesus our Lord.**

Believers have cast away their sin-nature and put Jesus on the throne of their lives and your eternal life has started. The Believers Born-again Spirit and "GOD, the Holy Spirit" are inside believers in a Temple not made with human hands.

Now let us continue the look at the life of the Patriarchs of the Bible.

How do Believers mentally process, King David's adultery and murder,

**with the righteousness given David
by GOD for David's love for GOD?**

What can we learn from all the missteps of the mighty men in the Bible; Moses killed a man out of anger, Abraham made many missteps, and King David seems a mess? In each case their "love for GOD" was considered to them as right-standing with GOD. What does GOD want us to receive from these three men and their stories and how might their stories apply to Believers lives in the New Covenant?

- Consider the problem facing Believers from the actions of King David; he committed adultery and murder and yet, having a heart for GOD; David's love and commitment to GOD, was counted as righteousness for David?
- David knew he was acting against GOD and when he strayed from the truth, he recognized his missteps, repented, and regained his focus for his relationship with GOD. David chronicled his repentance to GOD, for forgetting who he was, and what he stood for as a child of GOD, in Psalm 51.

What is the correct fact based, biblically contextual picture of GOD's ability within GOD's own rules to count the Patriarchs love and commitment as rightstanding with GOD?

- How can a correct picture of "GOD" be deduced by Believers considering David's murder and adultery, when Believers have an inculcated mindset of the ten Commandments; that breaking the commandments identifies sin? Breaking the commandments is sin but the Patriarch's sins or lawlessness is not the sin that separates you from GOD.

- **Believers have misled themselves, trying to live within the Ten Commandments, when GOD's purpose for the Commandments was to identify mankind's need for a Savior.** The sin that separates anyone from GOD is to reject Jesus from being the GOD of your life and living your life worshipping yourself.

Important note: Believers acting from a heartfelt motivation of love for GOD and love for your neighbor are fulfilling the Lord's will and destiny for Believers.

- What is the correct fact based biblically contextual picture of sin? Answer: There is only one sin that leads to death and that sin is to live unto yourself and reject the "love of" and your "need for" the Savior, Jesus Christ.
- Lawlessness or actions against the instructions in The Ten Commandments have devastating consequences down to every hurtful word or thought, but a Believers lawlessness will not ruin your relationship with GOD but acting lawlessly will leave deep scars from the consequences.

Foundational note; **Jesus Christ died for the redemption of the entire world and everyone that has ever lived or will live; and each person who ever lived or will live is** recorded in the "Lambs Book of Life" and is redeemed if they choose to receive the Lord's redemption. The only way to have your name blotted out of the "Lambs Book of Life" is to live for yourself and reject Jesus Christ as Savior. Listen to these words of Jesus.

> **Revelation 3:5** The one who conquers will be clothed thus in white garments, and **I will never blot his name out of the book of life.** I will confess his name before my Father and before his angels.

Now back to King David, Moses and Abraham and their connection to the Salvation of GOD. Although their love and commitment to God was counted as righteousness, there were consequences for Patriarchs works of the flesh, below is a list of consequences to David's adultery and murder:

> his son from the adulterous relationship died,
> his children fought and killed each other over the throne of David,
> David **did not** get to build The Temple for GOD, and
> David spent several years without the personal relationship with GOD **that he wanted.**

Listen as David pours out his heart to GOD repenting for taking Bathsheba and killing her husband Uriah.

> **Psalms 51:1-4** Have mercy on me, O God, according to your steadfast love; according to your abundant mercy **blot out my transgressions. Wash me thoroughly from my iniquity, and**

cleanse me from my sin! For I know my transgressions, and my sin is ever before me. **Against you, you only, have I sinned** and done what is evil in your sight, so that you may be justified in your words and blameless in your judgment.

Notice: David did not consider his sin against Bathsheba and her husband as sin against the Ten Commandments, but his sin was only against his relationship with GOD. How can this be? David understood his salvation was GOD's salvation, in the Spiritual world, and knew that GOD's salvation was from **outside time** (Where GOD is) because Jesus Christ sacrifice had not happened yet, in earthly time, but had happened in GOD's time. Jesus died for the sins of the entire world from the beginning of time to the end of time.

Notice in the next scripture; David was blessed with the Holy Spirit as a seal of GOD's salvation. David needed his iniquities against his relationship with GOD absolved by GOD. So, David is <u>speaking</u> his repentance and is desperate to repair his relationship with GOD. A few verses after David's cry for repentance and asking for forgiveness, David ask for a <u>clean heart, continued presence of the Holy Spirit, and the joy of **GOD's salvation**</u>.

Psalms 51:10-12 **Create in me a clean heart,** O God, and **renew a right spirit within me. Cast me not away from your presence,** <u>and take not your Holy Spirit from me. Restore to me the joy **of your salvation,**</u> and uphold me with a willing spirit.

Note; Feel the passion in this verse, Almighty GOD considers this contrition as faith, when anyone wants to change the direction of their life and put Jesus on the throne of their life, and become a child of GOD they will be welcomed.

Meanwhile back to David, he received consequences for his man-made choices, to act outside the perfect love he experienced in his relationship with GOD, but his relationship with GOD did not fail from his missteps. Listen as David prophesies about GOD's desire and announces that David has and is willing to give what GOD desires for their personal relationship.

> Psalms 51:15-17 O Lord, open my lips, and my mouth will declare your praise. **For you will not delight in sacrifice, or I would give it; you will not be pleased with a burnt offering. The sacrifices of God are a broken spirit; a broken and contrite heart, O God, you will not despise.**

David brought GOD a contrite heart and a broken spirit as a sacrifice. As evidence of GOD's love for David, listen to the promise to Mary, the Mother of Jesus, describe the throne of David being for eternity.

> Luke 1:32-35 And the angel said to Mary, "Do not be afraid, Mary, for you have found favor with God. And behold, you will conceive in your womb and bear a son, and you shall call his name Jesus. He will be great and will be called the Son of the Most High. **And the Lord God will give to him the throne of his father David, and he will reign over**

the house of Jacob forever, and of his kingdom there will be no end."
If Jesus is to rule from the throne of David, we must assume that David's love relationship with GOD is more important to GOD than David's lawlessness. Let us examine more scripture. What are Believers to gain from David's story?

I suggest that the take-away is a Believer **MUST experience a broken spirit and contrite heart to exchange** living unto themselves **for living for and in a relationship with your Savior, Jesus Christ, through "GOD, the Holy Spirit"? Listen as the Apostle Paul explains the love relationship with Jesus Christ and Believers.**

> **Romans 12:1** I appeal to you therefore, brothers, by the mercies of God, to **present your bodies as a living sacrifice, holy and acceptable to God,** which is your spiritual worship. Do not be conformed to this world, but be transformed by the renewal of your mind, that by testing you may discern what is the will of God, what is good and acceptable and perfect.

As Believers, **our commitment** is to love Jesus and Father GOD, and "GOD, the Holy Spirit" with all our heart, mind, soul, and strength and love our neighbor as ourselves. It is "the act" of considering others more significantly than ourselves that keeps believers in the center of the will of a loving caring GOD.

The church has sadly missed the lesson of David's overarching love for GOD with the churches picture of behavioral repentance for lawlessness.

Behavioral repentance and religious principles are not what David used to find the joy of GOD's salvation. GOD desires Believers to walk in "love" honoring GOD and not falling prey to the missteps that will cause GOD's children pain. Remember, David brought a broken Spirit, a broken and contrite heart to GOD as his sacrifice for sin.

The Webster's dictionary says that repentance (Greek word, metanoia) is changing your mind, or changing your direction or turning around, or regret for actions or sin, but in the life of a Believer, **repentance is correcting and having the right mindset and knowing who you are in Christ Jesus. If your mind strays from the following facts, you must re-orient (change, repent) your mind to the TRUTH of your identity in Jesus Christ instantly, by capturing bad thoughts and casting them out and standing on who you are in Christ Jesus.**
Believers are the righteousness of GOD in Christ.
2nd Cor 5:21
Believers are sanctified.
Hebrews 10:10
Believers are redeemed.
Galatians 3:13
Believers are a child of the most-high GOD.
John 20:27
Believers have been justified.
1st Cor 6:11

Believers have the Temple of GOD inside you.
  1st Cor 3:16
Believers have the Fruit of the Spirit inside you.
  Galatians 5:22
Believers have the fulness of the Godhead inside.
  Colossians 2:9
Grace and peace are **multiplied**
  through the knowledge of Jesus Christ
  2nd Peter 1-2
GOD does not remember your sins and
  is merciful to your iniquities.
  Hebrews 8:12
If you **do not believe** any of these facts from GOD's word, you must repent or change your mind to the truth of your identity in Jesus Christ. Your spirit is made perfect by Jesus Christ from incorruptible seed. Repentance is not a onetime thing that you do when you put Jesus Christ on the "Throne of your life" but **it is also capturing and changing any and every thought** that comes against your **identity in Christ Jesus.**

God looks upon the Heart
For the revealing of the person's motivation.
Believers suffer from **not believing their own story of the redemption of sin by Jesus Christ** and the "Perfectness of the Believer's Spirit" that comes from GOD, remembering your sin no more. **If you don't believe in your complete and everlasting redemption you will not be able to repent to renew your mind to your identity in Christ Jesus.** Read these scriptures again and **notice that**

God, the Holy Spirit, 101

everything <u>Jesus has finished</u> for Believers is in the <u>past tense</u>. Believers have already inherited these accomplishments of Jesus Christ. Believers must move in the assurance that, the promises we have in Jesus Christ are 1992 years old but are active today, for the life issues that arise daily in the same way redemption was available for the Patriarchs.

Back to the Patriarchs, Believers may be asking yourself; How can David, Abraham, Moses, and a few more men and women <u>please GOD</u> and it be counted to them as righteousness? **The Answer is GOD looks upon the heart,** (Spirit) and when GOD finds singular focus of the heart of an individual   bent toward "GOD, the Father", it is accepted as worship and it is counted as righteousness. Abraham, Moses, and King David, all three had a pre-eminent relationship with GOD, that was before any other relationship in their lives. All three Patriarchs lived in the Spiritual Kingdom of GOD, talking to GOD Almighty and receiving communication in return. All three knew how to **"go out and come in",** to a personal relationship with GOD that was pre-eminent in their lives.

Remember the question is; How can these mighty men commit, what Christians think are horrendous sins and yet be considered righteous by GOD **before Jesus died** for the sin of the entire world? The answer is difficult, if you do not understand the Spiritual world, and <u>that the Spiritual world is outside time and that Jesus died for the Patriarch's sin also</u>. **GOD remembered the Patriarchs sin** no more and was merciful to their lawlessness before they committed the lawlessness, because these men loved GOD with all their heart, mind, soul, and strength. The Patriarchs received GOD's salvation (outside time), before Jesus had gone to the cross in earthly time.

Think about the Christian salvation; In a similar event "outside time" the Believer's sin **was forgiven by Jesus** before Believers were born, 1992 years ago at the cross. The Believers salvation and its benefits were in place for you to claim before you were born, and the Patriarchs were forgiven after they committed sin at the cross, similar to Believers receiving salvation outside time.

Now let us, listen to King David talking to Solomon, about how to act, as Solomon is given King David's throne. How can David make this statement in the light of his sins, but then concentrate on the Lord's words, "walk before me with faithfulness with all your heart and with all your soul" as David did?

David's Instructions to Solomon

> 1st Kings 2:1-4 When David's time to die drew near, he commanded Solomon his son, saying, "I am about to go the way of all the earth. Be strong, and show yourself a man, and keep the charge of the LORD your God, **walking in his ways and keeping his statutes, his commandments, his rules, and his testimonies**, as it is written in the Law of Moses, that you may prosper in all that you do and wherever you turn, **that the LORD may establish his word that he**

spoke concerning me, saying, 'If your sons pay close attention to *their way, to walk before me in faithfulness with all their heart and with all their soul*, you shall not lack a man on the throne of Israel.'

Now listen to Solomon inquiring of GOD to discover the key to King David's relationship with GOD, that Solomon realized but did not understand. What does it mean David knew, "how to go out and come in"?

Solomon's Prayer for Wisdom

> **1st Kings 3:7-11** At Gibeon the LORD appeared to Solomon in a dream by night, and God said, "Ask what I shall give you." And Solomon said, "You have shown great and steadfast love to your servant David my father, **because he walked before you in faithfulness, in righteousness, and in uprightness of heart toward you.** And **you have kept for him this great and steadfast love** and have given him a son to sit on his throne this day. And now, O LORD my God, you have made your servant king in place of David my father, although I am but a little child.
>
> **I do not know how**
> **"to go out or come in"** .
>
> And your servant is in the midst of your people whom you have chosen, a great people, too many to be numbered or counted for multitude. **Give your servant therefore an understanding mind to govern your people, that I may discern between good and evil, for who is able to govern**

this your great people?"
Again, we are confronted with GOD saying that David walked in GOD's ways and kept all GOD's statutes, **because he walked before GOD in faithfulness, in righteousness, and in uprightness of heart toward GOD** now the last promise for Solomon, GOD speaking;

> 1st Kings 3:13-14 I give you also what you have not asked, both riches and honor, so that no other king shall compare with you, all your days. And if **you will walk in my ways, keeping my statutes** and my commandments, **as your father David walked**, then I will **lengthen your days."**

The unfortunate end of Solomon is detailed again in this last scripture about the failing of Solomon to keep a perfect heart focused on GOD that David possessed.

> **1st Kings 11:4** And it cometh to pass, at the time of the old age of Solomon, his wives **have turned aside his heart after other gods**, and his heart **hath not** been perfect with **Jehovah his God, like the heart of David his father.**

Notice The uprightness of David's heart for GOD had made the lawlessness of David forgiven and not remembered but Solomon did not keep his heart focused toward GOD. The explanation of the perfectness of David's heart of love for GOD, **points out the pre-eminent focus of David** and the downfall of Solomon, who found other gods. Listen to the Apostle Paul as he tells Believers that before the foundation of time, all who believe are in Christ Jesus.

> Ephesians 1:3-4 Blessed be the God and Father

of our Lord Jesus Christ, <u>who hath blessed us with all spiritual blessings</u> in heavenly places in Christ: **According as he hath chosen us in him before the foundation of the world, that we should be holy and without blame before him in love:** Notice again, that all spiritual blessings **have been given** in the past tense, **Believers already have all the blessings of Jesus Christ.** <u>*You will not need blessings in Heaven.*</u>

Let us take a minute to discuss being "holy" the word means to be separated to GOD, David was separated to GOD, holy does not mean to try to live the Ten Commandments or a different lists of do's and don'ts from your church, **it means to love GOD with all your heart, mind, soul, and strength every second of your life.**

Now let us get back to this reference of relationship with GOD that David, Abraham, Moses and all Believers received to <u>"Go out and Come in"</u> to relationship with GOD.

What does, "Going out and coming in" indicate about a relationship with GOD?

Now let us look at Moses, who after forty years of leading Israel through the desert with GOD was denied entrance into the "Promised Land" because of the hitting the rock with his staff to produce water and killing of the Egyptian, out of anger, and without instruction. Moses committed the top sin to most everyone in the Church age and yet the murder did not restrict Moses from having an intimate relationship with GOD Almighty. Moses lawlessness **cost him** forty years in the desert and kept him from entering the promised land. **There are always consequences for man-made acts of lawlessness.** Listen to Moses handing leadership of Israel over to Joshua.

Joshua to Succeed Moses

Deuteronomy 31:1-4 And Moses went and spoke these words unto all Israel. And he said unto them, I am an hundred and twenty years old this day; *"I can "no more go out and come in"*: **also the LORD hath said unto me,** Thou shalt **not go** over this Jordan. **The LORD thy God, he will go over before thee, and he will destroy these nations from before thee, and thou shalt possess them:** *and* Joshua, he shall go over before thee, as the LORD hath said. And the LORD shall do unto them as he did to Sihon and to Og, kings of the Amorites, and unto the land of them, whom he destroyed.

Did you notice that Moses could no longer, **"go out and come in"** to the Lord for the people of Israel? All of the great men of GOD suffered loss for their misdeeds but kept their relationship with God by never faltering on their love for GOD and their pre-eminent relationship with GOD above all other relationships.

Listen to the following scriptures to become confident that Believers will always and forever be able to **"go out and come in"** to a relationship with GOD with our ability to enter and draw near to the Throne of grace:

> Hebrews 4:15 For we do not have a high priest who is unable to sympathize with our weaknesses, but one who in every respect has been tempted as we are, yet without sin. **Let us then with confidence draw near to the throne of grace,** that we may receive mercy and find grace to help in time of need.

Now, listen as the Psalmist promises that Believers can **"go out and come in" to GOD for evermore.**

My Help Comes from the Lord

Psalms 121:1-8 A Song of degrees.

I will lift up mine eyes unto the hills,
> from whence cometh my help.
>> My help cometh from the LORD,
>>> which made heaven and earth.
>> He will not suffer thy foot to be moved:
> he that keeps thee will not slumber.

Behold, he that keeps Israel
> shall neither slumber nor sleep.
>> The LORD is thy keeper:
>>> the LORD is thy shade
>>>> upon thy right hand.
>>> The sun shall not smite thee
>> by day, nor the moon by night.
> The LORD shall preserve thee from all evil:

he shall preserve thy soul.
>> **The LORD shall preserve**
>>> **"thy going out and thy coming in"**
>>> **from this time forth,**

God, the Holy Spirit, 108

and even for evermore.

And once more, listen to the Moses enumerate the promise of blessings that are available when you have an intense relationship with GOD Almighty and notice you will be blessed coming in or going out.

> **Deuteronomy 28:1-6** And it shall come to pass, if you shall hearken diligently unto the voice of the LORD thy God, to observe and to do all his commandments which I command thee this day, that the LORD thy God will set thee on high above all nations of the earth: **And all these blessings shall come on thee, and overtake thee, if you** shall hearken unto the voice of the LORD thy God. Blessed shalt thou be **in the city,** and blessed shalt thou be **in the field**. Blessed *shall be* **the fruit of thy body,** and the **fruit of thy ground,** and the **fruit of thy cattle,** the increase of thy kine, and the flocks of thy sheep. Blessed shall be **thy basket and thy store. Blessed shalt thou be when thou "come in, and blessed shalt thou be when thou go out".**

Notice; the Blessings verse starts with **"if you",** fortunately "If you" does not apply to Believers because of what "Jesus **"has done"** and the blessing verse finishes announcing the Believers ability to always be blessed when Believers, **"come in and go out"** with GOD, our Father, Jesus Christ our Redeemer, and "GOD, the Holy Spirit".

Let us take a minute to refresh our understanding of the New Covenant in Hebrews 8 and 10 to see the connection.

Hebrews 8:7-12 For if that **first covenant had been faultless,** there would have been no occasion to look for a second (covenant). For he finds fault with them when he says: "Behold, the days are coming, declares the Lord, when **"I will" establish a new covenant** with the house of Israel (Jews) and with the house of Judah (Gentiles) , not like the covenant that I made with their fathers on the day when I took them by the hand to bring them out of the land of Egypt. For they did not continue in my covenant, and so I showed no concern for them, declares the Lord. **For this is the covenant that I will make with the house of Israel after those days, declares the Lord: I will put my laws into their minds, and write them on their hearts, and I will be their God, and they shall be my people.** And they shall not teach, each one his neighbor and each one his brother, saying, 'Know the Lord,' for they shall all know me, from the least of them to the greatest. **For I will be merciful toward their iniquities, and I will remember their sins no more."** In speaking of a new covenant, he makes the first one obsolete. And what is becoming obsolete and growing old is ready to vanish away.

Notice; GOD gave you His word with five "I wills" and one "they shall" promises to replace the "If you do good, you receive good and if you do bad, you receive bad" covenant. Re-read Hebrews 8:7-12 and Hebrews 10:12-18 if you did not deposit the "I will" and "they shall" promises in your heart.

The sacrifice of Jesus Christ went forward to include believers in the present day but also included Believers from before the Lord's birth from the beginning of time to the end of time. If Believers are not able to realize that the Lord Jesus Christ sacrifice, **is outside time,** Believers will only have hope for salvation, **instead of faith.** Without true faith in the sacrifice, death, and resurrection of the Lord, Believers will not be able to appropriate the promises of Father GOD and the Lord Jesus. The promises of GOD are finished, and the inheritance of the saints is available to those that believe and act with their faith **speaking** the change in their heart.

Listen to the promise of the inheritance to the Saints from the Lord;

Inheritance of the Saints; Imagine,

The Lord's blood redeemed the Believers sin,

    His stripes healed our diseases,

        on His shoulders He bore our sorrows

        and carried our griefs,

    He was pierced for our transgressions,

    His body was bruised for our iniquities,

He was punished to bring us peace, and

    He was made poor that we might become rich.

        Isaiah 53 and 2nd Corinthians 9:8-11

Remember; The gifts and promises of GOD are not yours until they are unwrapped and used.

GOD has <u>not put any</u> obstructions
between Believers and Himself,
except to believe GOD loves Believers.

The principles of Christianity without a full-on relationship with GOD **will not** yield the divine results, Believers may be looking to enjoy. Christians can live in wishing and hoping that they have a relationship with GOD, but Christians must believe in GOD's love for Believers for GOD to consider the belief as faith. The root word for faith is trust and the root word for trust is true. GOD is both trustworthy and is truth.

Personal performance to obtain anything form GOD is a failed plan,

> The saving prayer, baptism, tithing, Sunday school, Sunday services, faith, grace, acts of kindness, holiness and many more actions are great practices and principles to do and study, but **Jesus died to reconcile mankind to GOD and give Believers "GOD, the Holy Spirit" to be inside you for a personal relationship. Your relationship with GOD needs to be the pre-eminent relationship in your life and it must be based on what Jesus has done not what you can do.**

Do not allow yourself to be stuck and stranded in Religion; Christianity is not a religion but **a personal relationship with a living GOD,** which means a loving, caring, two-way communication with GOD. A fulltime, **intimate,** intense relationship with GOD is the only way you can love GOD with all your heart, mind, soul, and strength and love others more significantly than yourself. The mechanics of Christianity are good, but mechanics or principles **will not** replace a pre-eminent one-on-one relationship with GOD.

Faith works **by the love Believers have for GOD and by the grace** GOD has for Believers. **The Believers actions need to be "born" out of the intimacy with "GOD, the Holy Spirit".** Did you noticed the use of the word "intimate and born" in describing the Believers relationship with GOD, God is love and if you have a relationship with GOD it must be a loving, caring, intimate relationship so that your words and actions are born out of the relationship of "Love". Do you know and believe GOD loves you? The Apostle Paul warns mankind that Believers must honor GOD as GOD. What is your picture of Honoring GOD? Listen to the Apostle Paul;

> Romans 1:21-25 For although they knew God, they **did not honor him as** God or give thanks to him, but they became futile in their thinking, and their foolish hearts were darkened. Claiming to be wise, they became fools, and exchanged the glory of the immortal God for images resembling mortal man and birds and animals and creeping things. Therefore God gave them up in the lusts of their hearts to impurity, to the dishonoring of their bodies among themselves, **because they exchanged the truth about God for a lie and worshiped and served the creature rather than the Creator,** who is blessed forever! Amen.

God, the Holy Spirit, 113

Revelation 4:11 "Worthy are you, our Lord and God, **to receive glory and honor and power, for you created all things, and by your will they existed and were created.**"
Psalms 32:8-10 **I will instruct you and teach you in the way you should go; I will counsel you with my eye upon you.** Be not like a horse or a mule, without understanding, which must be curbed with bit and bridle, or it will not stay near you. Many are the sorrows of the wicked, **but steadfast love surrounds the one who trusts in the LORD.**

Honoring GOD is to love GOD with all your heart, mind, soul, and strength and to love your neighbor as yourself. **Repentance is changing any thought in your mind to the truth and authority of your relationship with GOD Almighty, Jesus Christ, and "GOD, the Holy Spirit".**

Believers cannot be an old sinner saved by grace. You are either a sinner or **you are not.** Lawlessness is a litany of bad acts, but sin is **NOT** choosing Jesus Christ to be on the "Throne" of your life", so that the Spirit of Jesus Christ can abide with you. Mankind and Believers have either put the Lord Jesus Christ on the throne of your life **and are saved** or you are living unto yourself and that is the sin unto death. The Sunday only Christian will go to Heaven but may live with terrible man-made results without any of the incredible "abundant life" Jesus died to bring to Believers.

The Believers relationship with GOD is a Spiritual relationship, attenuated by your faith to explore the grace of GOD available to affect your physical relationship with the world, with the power of the Spirit. **GOD does not** move in your life according to your performance (flesh) but according to your love for, and trust in GOD.

Listen as the Apostle Paul instructs.

> **The law was given to give sin power over mankind to destroy their self-righteousness and reveal their need for a Savior. Galatians 3:10-14 and Romans 14:23 Believers can have an incorrect concept of GOD, colored by consequences of sin instead of GOD's love for mankind.**
>
> Galatians 2:16 Knowing that a man **is not** justified by the works of the law, but by the faith of Jesus Christ, **even we have believed in Jesus Christ, that we might be justified by the faith of Christ,** and not by the works of the law: for by the works of the law **shall no flesh be justified.**

Conclusion, When Believers look at the love for GOD that King David, Moses, and Abraham developed with GOD, do you realize that it is your relationship and love for GOD that needs to be paramount in your life. Believers are not defined by your mistakes or your good deeds; **you are defined by your love relationship with GOD. In regard to sin, Believers must quit remembering what GOD has forgotten and concentrate on your relationship with GOD, through "GOD, the Holy Spirit".**

God, the Holy Spirit, 116

The Journey to discover "God, the Holy Spirit".

Chapter 5

How can considering others more significantly than yourself be GOD's destiny for Believers?

GOD is love and love is considering others more significantly than yourself. Jesus gave us the example of love by laying down His life for the world. Now, as Believers, who have freely received GOD's love, let us freely give of ourselves to GOD who loved us first. Our heritage, from a loving GOD, is to love GOD and those in need. **The constant motivation** to act for the benefit of others is a picture of the love GOD has for Believers. Acts of kindness brings glory to our Savior. It is the Believer's transformation from living unto yourself to **living for GOD** that differentiates Believers from those not yet committed to Jesus Christ, Father GOD, and embracing the gift of "GOD, the Holy Spirit". Loving yourself before GOD and others is idolatry.

If your daily plans and momentary ideas **are not** born out of an intimate relationship with GOD to plan and execute your daily actions, you will be **living without** the wisdom and provision from "GOD, the Holy Spirit". Therefore, your plans and your results will be man-made. **"GOD, the Holy Spirit" is the essence of the New Covenant,** that **Jesus died to give Believers.** This fact must change the Believers perception; from Father GOD is in Heaven and Jesus is at His right Hand; to "GOD, the Holy Spirit" is inside the Believers. Believers have eternal life and are part of GOD's family, right now, on Earth. Listen to GOD's promise and realize the fallacy of living in your own power.

And **God is able to make all grace**
> abound to you,
>> so that having **all sufficiency**
>>> **in all things**
>>>> **at all times,**
>>>>> you may abound
>>>>> in every good work.
>>>>> **2nd Corinthians 9:8**

Any acts of kindness you are giving away to others, in personal time or substance, is part of GOD's world. Considering others more significantly than yourself is the first step to having "GOD, the Holy Spirit" approve a plan and provide divine supply necessary for treating others more significantly than yourself. **"GOD, the Holy Spirit" is wanting to give you a word of knowledge for everyone destined to be in your path today.** All acts of kindness, from a heart filled with love, bring glory to GOD; from you and from the recipient of the kindness. Compassion for others starts **the invisible world of GOD's grace** from your **invisible born-again Spirit** wrapped in **invisible love from the Spirit of GOD, for the Believers visible action of kindness for the benefit of others.**

Do not make Earth your home.

Love GOD by spending time with GOD relating to your life, find your way to live inside the invisible, but very real world of the Spirit. Focusing on being a steward of GOD's world instead of working for ownership of your own world. "GOD, the Holy Spirit" is a Spirit personification and Believers must use faith methods to communicate. Constantly ask questions about anything, about the Bible, and about opportunities to bless others and then be quiet to allow "GOD, the Holy Spirit" to bring a thought or scripture to your mind that will express the leading or conclusion. "GOD, the Holy Spirit" is a Spirit and therefore communicates with your Spirit and Believers must hear "GOD, the Holy Spirit" through faith in your mind. The more you learn the language of love from GOD, the more often you will hear "GOD, the Holy Spirit".

At first, learning to trust the non-verbal communications with GOD is difficult because you have to hear the communication by faith.

When Believers choose an action from the compassion in your heart, you can have confidence in your action. When Believers bring the plan for action for approval to "GOD, the Holy Spirit" He will make provision for the kindness, that GOD may receive glory for the act of kindness. The more of GOD's word you have stored up in your heart will help you confirm hearing from "GOD, the Holy Spirit".

Now a personal story, approximately 10 years ago, I was praying hard to hear from GOD and receive direction in how I could be used to further the Kingdom of GOD. The answer in my Spirit was to write something. I have never been celebrated as a wordsmith or a person with great grammar, but I knew I had a word from the Lord, then I discovered GOD was not going to tell me what to write or what subject to write about? The walk of faith was and still is by the minute with my constant question as to which path to follow. The solid rock upon which I move in faith must be motivated by love for GOD and for the benefit of others. The constant battle is to not allow a writing accomplishment to become prideful or have an agenda. The word of GOD must have voice, or it will **not** benefit others, my words not tagged onto the words from "GOD, the Holy Spirit" will only yield man-made thoughts. It is the knowledge of my Savior and new communication and relationship with "GOD, the Holy Spirit" that allows me to write something that will inspire someone to love GOD and experience the love of GOD in return. It takes a constant mental analysis of the indications in my Spirit to weigh the alternatives and to get a confirmation from "GOD, the Holy Spirit" as to which thought, or subject is right and then I must act in faith believing the choice. After many years I can see that the alternatives that come to mind in my Spirit are more Intune with love and all the fruit of the Spirit and therefore keep me in peace, (shalom) that my thoughts are positive to helping Believers and others.

Lean not to your own understanding,
But constantly communicate with your Spirit
and "GOD, the Holy Spirit".

Listen to Jesus tell Believers of the power, "GOD, the Holy Spirit" will bring to the Believer's life by leading Believers into all truth and telling believers things happening in the future.

> John 16:13 When the <u>Spirit of truth</u> comes, **he will guide you into all the truth,** for he will not speak on his own authority, but whatever he hears he will speak, and **he will declare to you the things that are to come**.

<u>Note of comfort</u>; A Believer cannot go wrong when sincerely acting on a word from your faith in GOD even if it is misplaced and not quite heard correctly. GOD is with you and a thought based on love and for the benefit of others cannot go terribly wrong. The overriding principle is that your act of kindness is not for your own benefit.

> **Do not miss the importance of**
> **knowing things to come,**
> **GOD's grace is acting on a word from GOD.**

Knowing things to come is so important to planning your day, your next moment, and identifies the importance of an intimate relationship with "GOD, the Holy Spirit". When a Believer depends on asking, "GOD, the Holy Spirit" for **what is to come:** in your family, your work, and in the next room you enter. The Believer can be ready to minister to a person in need of salvation, healing, deliverance, an encouraging word, or provision; if you have faith in "GOD, the Holy Spirit" and communicate with the Holy Spirit to know what is coming next.

> **1st Corinthians 14:1** Follow after charity and desire spiritual things, but rather that you may prophesy.

To prophesy, is to encourage and when prompted by

"GOD, the Holy Spirit", insight into the person needing encouragement is available.
Warning, The Believer will always know, if the prompting to encourage becomes critical or judgmental, **it is not from the Lord.**

Believers are GOD's hands, legs, and banks on earth for ministering acts of kindness for others. Remember; **Father GOD and Jesus Christ are "finished", and Believers are in the era of "GOD, the Holy Spirit" and the Holy Spirit era is the greatest era of all time.** This is the first time that Father GOD can have a personal relationship with every Believer, since the Garden of Eden. Believers must develop their personal mechanism to hear the words of the "Holy Spirit of GOD" and act on the word of GOD, in faith, that you heard the Lord correctly. Learning to trust that you have heard a word from GOD is difficult at first and humbles you until you realize that the only way to be sure you heard the Lord correctly is to make sure that the foundation of your motivation is for others and motivated by love.

There are two parts to the New Creation Life, one is an intimate loving caring relationship with GOD, and the second, is always considering others more significantly than ourselves. Can you see that loving GOD and others more significantly than your self is an example of perfect love because there is no selfishness?

Thinking of others more significantly than your self is not easy, but as we receive the love GOD has for Believers and accept stewardship of God's world as Believers destiny, we can experience the nature of GOD as we give to others. **Believers are living in the world but are not subject to the culture of personal accomplishments for success, but instead Believers are living to celebrate GOD's accomplishments.** Listen to the Apostle Paul as he tells Believers about our lives with "GOD, the Holy Spirit".

Ephesians 3:14-21 For this reason I bow my knees before the Father from whom **every family in heaven and on earth is named,** that according to the riches of his glory he may grant you to be **strengthened with power through his Spirit in your inner being,** so that Christ may dwell in your hearts through faith—that you, **being rooted and grounded in love,** may have strength to comprehend with all the saints what is the **breadth** and **length** and **height** and **depth,** and **to know the love of Christ that surpasses knowledge, *that you may be filled with all the fullness of God.***

If being filled with the fullness of GOD isn't too overwhelming, now think about this next thought of the power at work within us to bring glory to Jesus Christ.

Ephesians 3:17-19 Now to him who is able to do far more abundantly than all that we (Believers) ask or think, according to the power at work within us, to him be glory in the church and in Christ Jesus throughout all generations, forever and ever. Amen.

Read this scripture several times until you grasp the full measure of GOD's love and power available to Believers being filled with the fullness of GOD.

Below is a list of other scriptures and the promise attached to them.

- This new era of GOD is Believers being led by the word of GOD and "GOD, the Holy Spirit" from inside the Believer. 1st Corinthians 6:16
- **The Believer** has been **made** righteous and sin will not be imputed to the account of the believer. Hebrews 8:12 and 10:17
- **The new era** with "GOD, the Holy Spirit" is one of action in "The Name of Jesus". Colossians 3:17
- **Experiencing the complexity of every Creation of GOD** and having your eyes open to visualizing GOD Almighty and Jesus Christ in everything you see brings the joy of the Lord and shalom to the Believers life. Romans 8:31-39
- **The Believer's** life is lived from the victory of Jesus, **not** looking to be victorious for the Lord Jesus. Ephesians 4:4
- **The authority** of the believer is delivered by faith filled words without doubt, activated with the love we have through Jesus Christ and his sacrifice of love for Believers and others. Matthew 21:21

The everyday use of faith from a word from "GOD, the Holy Spirit", and the love in Believers hearts for GOD builds confidence to conquer unbelief when it appears. (1st John 5:14)

GOD's love for Believers was shown 1992 years ago
When He wrote your name in the,
"Lamb's book of Life".

All the promises of Jesus have been waiting on Believers 1,992 years. Your name **was not** written in "The Lamb's Book of Life" when you believed, your name was already there. Remember; "Jesus died once for all mankind" meaning from the beginning of time to the end of time. When you, as a Believer, accepted the salvation offered by Jesus Christ, the salvation and all its benefits have been waiting for believers their entire life.

When you believed in the victory of Jesus 1,992 years ago and desired to get right with GOD, your belief appropriated **(claimed)** your New Creation Spirit from the cross. Actions and promises of the Lord **are not** bound by time or space; for if the promises were time sensitive, Believers could not be redeemed, delivered, healed, sanctified, or made perfect in righteousness. **Right-standing with GOD is the most powerful thing on Earth and its origin is outside time and space but is inside every Believer filled with "GOD, the Holy Spirit".**

Listen again, as I say the same thing in a different way; **A Believer's faith will not move Father GOD;** Father GOD and Jesus Christ have already moved.

So how can mankind get anything from the death and Resurrection of Jesus Christ from 1992 years ago?

God, the Holy Spirit, 125

Jesus died for your sin, was resurrected for your salvation and its benefits before you were born. Listen to the promise to receive salvation and it benefits from 1992 years ago.

> Romans 10:9-10 That if thou shalt **confess with thy mouth** the Lord Jesus and shall believe in thine heart that God **hath** raised him from the dead, (1992 years ago) thou shalt be saved. For with the heart man believeth unto righteousness; and with **the mouth confession is made unto salvation.**

Note: When unbelievers put Jesus on the throne of their life, the New Christians have not accomplished anything to deserve GOD's grace. The unbeliever was not a tither, did not go to church, did not teach Sunday school, was not living holy, but **GOD loved the unbeliever** while they were yet the god of their life. Now salvation and all of its benefits are the Believers possession, right now, on earth without the Believer deserving or having earned GOD's grace, GOD's grace was a gift. In that same manner the benefits of Salvation are available without the Believer meriting the promises of GOD. Remember; Faith worketh through love for GOD and others.

Your relationship with GOD must be intense.

The word "intimate" is the Greek translation for the word used in the expression "know GOD". **Your relationship with GOD needs to be intimate and intense because the Believers actions need to be born out of this relationship with GOD.** GOD's love, the Lord's peace and wellbeing, has been stored up waiting on Believers to believe and bring voice to their inheritance from Jesus Christ. Listen to the confirmation from the Apostle Paul:

> Romans 7:4 Likewise, my brothers, you also have died to the law through the body of Christ, **so that you may belong to another,** to him (Jesus) who has been raised from the dead, **in order that we may bear fruit for God.**
>
> Romans 7:6 But now we are **released from the law,** having died to that which held us captive, so that we serve in the new way of **the Spirit** you. and **not in the old way** of the written code.

"GOD, the Holy Spirit" operates in the Spiritual Kingdom of GOD with your Born-again Spirit to change the visible world with the power of the Spiritual World. "GOD, the Holy Spirit" will only lead you to do things He has seen the Father and the Son do and say. Listen to Jesus confirm this statement.

> **John 5:19** So Jesus said to them, "Truly, truly, I say to you, the Son can do nothing of his own accord, but only what he sees the Father doing. For whatever the Father does, that the Son does likewise. **For the Father loves the Son and shows him all that he himself is doing.** And greater works than these will he show him, so that you may marvel. **For as the Father raises the dead and gives them life, so also the Son gives life to whom he will.**

When it is said that Jesus can "do nothing" of himself, it means that such is the union between the Father and the

Son, joined together before action. Such is the nature of the New Covenant union between the Believer and "GOD, the Holy Spirit", the Believer can "do nothing" that will bring glory to GOD without faith in "GOD, the Holy Spirit". Remember; it is not you doing the works, but GOD doing the acts of kindness through Believers.

Consume yourself with the family business,
Giving away God's love to others.

"The Law was given through Moses, grace and truth came by Jesus Christ." John 1:17 **Jesus is Grace and Truth.** Grace and Truth is the Spiritual world and Believers must grow to understand that the visible world came from the invisible world, "spoken" into existence by God. Notice the word "spoken" just as your salvation is spoken to reveal what is in your heart. (Romans 10:9-10) Listen to these two scriptures revealing the power of GOD's word spoken to add faith to belief.

> **John 1:1** In the beginning was the Word, and the Word was with God, and the Word was God. He (Jesus) was in the beginning with God. All things were made through him, and without him was not anything made that was made.
> Hebrews 11:3 By faith we understand that the **universe was created by the word of God,** _so that what is seen was not made out of things that are visible._

Now let us look at scriptures declaring Jesus as the High Priest of the Believer's words and their effect on the visible world from the power of GOD.

Hebrews 3:1-2 Wherefore, holy brethren, partakers of the heavenly calling, **consider the Apostle and High Priest of our (Believers confession) profession, Christ Jesus.**

Hebrews 3:6 but **Christ is faithful over God's house as a son.** And we are his house if indeed we hold fast our confidence and our boasting (speaking) in our hope.

Hebrews 4:14 **Seeing then that we have a great high priest, that is passed into the heavens,** Jesus the Son of God, let us hold fast our (confession) profession. Greek word (homo logia) meaning confession professed.

Jesus is the High Priest of our words, confessed for the benefits of others. When speaking a word from "GOD, the Holy Spirit" or a promise from the Bible "GOD, the Holy Spirit" will give substance to the word of God spoken to bring it to pass. That is confirmed with these three passages about Jesus. Now listen to one more scripture to build your confidence in speaking what you believe.

Matthew 21:21-22 Jesus answered and said unto them, Verily I say unto you, If ye have faith, and doubt not, ye shall **not only** do this which is done to the fig tree, but also **if ye shall say unto this mountain, Be thou removed, and be thou cast into the sea; it shall be done.** And all things, whatsoever ye shall **ask in prayer, believing,** ye shall receive.

Think about this; Faith annihilates time and space. To the

Believers faith, the unseen world of GOD's word, is more real than the seen world; and the distant as near as the things that can be touched. Faith spoken words from a compassionate heart appropriates and takes grace from the hand of God. But works of faith are impossible apart from the grace filled relationship with "GOD, the Holy Spirit". A Believers faith and knowledge, with proper motivation **will move the Believer into position to appropriate what GOD did at Creation and Jesus, the Redeemer provided 1992 years ago at the cross, through the power of "GOD, the Holy Spirit".**

Listen to your appointment to be an Ambassador for Jesus Christ.

> **2nd Corinthians 5:20-21 Therefore, we are ambassadors for Christ,** God making his appeal through us. We implore you on behalf of Christ, be reconciled to God. For our sake he made him to be sin who knew no sin, so that in him we might become the righteousness of God.

Does it get any better than this scripture?

Let us look at the scriptures to understand more about the Spiritual world and know how it affects Believers in our daily life? The three main elements to the post-cross life in the Kingdom of GOD are; acting in faith through love, communicating with GOD for the benefit of others, and participating in a relationship with "GOD, the Holy Spirit" to complete our destiny to bring glory to GOD.

The benefits of Salvation and all the promises of Jesus Christ are 1992 years old and must be grasped, so that you can establish belief in the promises. **Remember;**

when you believed for salvation and its benefits and put Jesus on the throne of your life, you had not tithed, been to a Wednesday service, taught Sunday School or anything to deserve the Gift of Jesus Christ except you believed that you needed a Savior. A Believer cannot make yourself worthy or do anything to earn the grace of GOD for any of the benefits of salvation, such as deliverance, healing, or provision except you believe and have a relationship with "GOD, the Holy Spirit" these benefits are the Believers blessing.

Listen to David in Psalm 103:

> **Psalm 103:2** Bless the LORD, O my soul, and **forget not all his benefits,** who forgives all your iniquity, who heals all your diseases, who redeems your life from the pit, who crowns you with steadfast love and mercy, who satisfies you with good so that your youth is renewed like the eagle's.

Living in the realm of the Kingdom of GOD in the Spiritual world and not forgetting GOD's benefits to Believers is the door to living the abundant life. Believe it, receive it, and act on your belief concentrating on benefiting others more significantly than yourself. The reason Paul said, "Do everything in word and deed all in the Name of Jesus" demonstrated that the motivation for your actions are heartfelt and not self-serving. (Colossians 3:16-17) "GOD, the Holy Spirit" has a plan for your good; can you hear "GOD, the Holy Spirit" telling you about the plan and are you ready to act and to speak it into existence?

A small example: **"GOD did not give you a Spirit of fear**

but of love, power, and a sound mind.",

2nd Timothy 1:7 For God hath not given us the spirit of fear; **but of power, and of love, and of a sound mind.**

The Believer must **believe and voice** that the Believer **will not receive fear** but will live in love, power, with a sound mind. Belief and voice activation is how the Spiritual world springs to life. It is difficult to think a bad thought away **but taking control of a thought by speaking GOD's promise will destroy contradictions to GOD's word when bad thoughts arise.** "GOD, the Holy Spirit", inside you will, activate the substance of the words. Remember, GOD made the words and when they are voiced **with the standing a Believer has in Christ Jesus** the words will perform their function. If you command fear to leave your mind and embrace your position in Jesus Christ, the spirit of fear will leave, and the peace of the Lord will remain.

GOD has a plan for your life
Today and every day.

GOD has a plan for your life, minute by minute, but you may not be following the plan or inquiring of GOD to understand the plan. GOD made a plan for the habitat of man and created the Earth. GOD wanted beauty and made flowers and tree, sunsets and stars. GOD made a plan for procreation and made mankind's body and created man and woman. God made a plan for your redemption and Jesus wrote your name in the "Lambs book of Life". GOD sent the Lord Jesus and Jesus has finished his planned sacrifice and has sent "GOD, the Holy Spirit" to Believers for comfort and power.

(The next part of the plan.) **God has given mankind control over your choice to act in concert with "GOD, the Holy Spirit" or to choose man-made actions.** GOD has given mankind a choice and even told mankind the best path; GOD said, "Choose life" with GOD.

Look at these three Old Testament and one New Testament scriptures to understand the expected results from living a man-made plan for your life or choosing a GOD centered life.

> Psalm 78:35 **They remembered that God was their rock, the Most High God their redeemer.** But they flattered him with their mouths; they lied to him with their tongues. **Their heart was not steadfast toward him;** they were **not** faithful to his covenant. Yet he, (GOD) being compassionate, atoned for their iniquity and did not destroy them; he restrained his anger often and did not stir up all his wrath. He (GOD) remembered that they were but flesh, a wind that passes and comes not again. How often they rebelled against him in the wilderness and grieved him in the desert! **They tested God again and again and provoked the Holy One of Israel.** They did not remember his power or the day when he redeemed them from the foe, when he performed his signs in Egypt and his marvels in the fields of Zoan.

Even in the Old Testament, following GOD was available

and GOD would deliver peace and prosperity. Listen as David tells us of his relationship with GOD.

Psalms 23:1 A Psalm of David. The LORD is **my shepherd;** I shall not want. He makes green pastures for me to lie down in. He leads me beside still waters. He restores my soul. He leads me in paths of righteousness for his name's sake. Even though **I walk** through the valley of the **shadow** of death, I will fear no evil, for you are with me; your rod and your staff, **they comfort me.** You prepare a table before me in the presence of my enemies; you anoint my head with oil; my cup overflows. Surely **goodness and mercy shall follow me all the days of my life, and I shall dwell in the house of the LORD forever.**

Notice: this Psalm is for Believers who choose the Lord as your shepherd; **Believers shall not want;** concentrate on I shall not want. There is a place in your life with "GOD, the Holy Spirit" as your shepherd that you can live in supply from GOD, for your needs, wants, and benefits, but you must follow the Shepherd and believe. GOD is not a respecter of persons.

Jeremiah 29:11 For I know the plans I have for you, declares the LORD, plans for welfare and not for evil, to give you a future and a hope. Then you will call upon (GOD) me and come and pray to me, and **I will** hear you. You will **seek (GOD) me and find me, when you seek me with all your heart. I will** be found by you, declares the LORD, and **I will** restore your fortunes and gather you from all the nations and all the places where I have driven you, declares the LORD, and **I will** bring you back to the place from which I sent you into exile.

GOD has made commitments to those who will seek the Kingdom of GOD first.

Matthew 6:19-21 "Do not lay up for yourselves treasures on earth, where moth and rust destroy and where thieves break in and steal, **but lay up for yourselves treasures in heaven,** where neither moth nor rust destroys and where thieves do not break in and steal. **For where your treasure is, there your heart will be also.**

Matthew 6:31 Therefore do not be anxious, saying, 'What shall we eat?' or 'What shall we drink?' or 'What shall we wear?' For the Gentiles seek after all these things, and your heavenly Father knows that you need them all. **But seek first the kingdom of God and his righteousness, and all these things will be added to you.**

Whether Old Testament or New Testament, it is mankind's responsibility to choose whom you will follow and whom or what you will worship with consequences for your choice.

The important connection to GOD's grace is right standing with GOD and love for GOD; Believers can steward all the inheritance of GOD and Jesus Christ for the benefit of others at the behest of "GOD, the Holy Spirit" including miracles. **GOD has not changed, GOD is the same** yesterday, today, and forever and GOD is a miracle working GOD. Surely salvation is a miracle, and much more difficult than a healing or deliverance or a provision opportunity.

Believers cannot live the life given by Jesus Christ Without "GOD, the Holy Spirit".
The plan of GOD for the Believer is completely dependent on a Believers relationship with "GOD, the Holy Spirit". Think about it; If "GOD, the Holy Spirit" is your shepherd, you shall not lack. The following scriptures are in context and speak to the importance of Believers understanding the role of "GOD, the Holy Spirit" as the gift of Jesus Christ as a seal of the Believers inheritance of all that Jesus accomplished for Believers. Believers have the power and the comfort from a daily personal relationship with the Holy Spirit of God abiding with and in every Believer baptized with "GOD, the Holy Spirit". The following scriptures highlight the importance of depending on the Holy Spirit every minute of every day.
Behold, the Lamb of God
John 1:29 **The next day** John, the Baptist, saw Jesus coming toward him, and said, "Behold, the Lamb of God, who takes away the sin of the world! This is he of whom I said, 'After me comes a man who ranks before me, because he was before me.' I myself did not know him, but for this purpose I came baptizing with water, that he might be revealed to Israel." And John bore witness: **"I saw the Spirit descend from heaven**

like a dove, and it remained on him. I myself did not know him, but he who sent me to baptize with water said to me, 'He on whom you see the Spirit descend and remain, this is he who baptizes with the Holy Spirit.' **And I have seen and have borne witness that this is the Son of God."**
GOD sent the Holy Spirit to be on and in Jesus before he performed one miracle. If it was important to Jesus to be baptized with the Spirit of GOD before he started His ministry, it is important to Believers? Therefore, every Believer should follow the example and be baptized in and with "GOD, the Holy Spirit".

John 14:9 **Jesus said to him,** "Have I been with you so long, and you still do not know me, Philip? Whoever has seen me has seen the Father. How can you say, 'Show us the Father'? **Do you not believe that I am in the Father and the Father is in me?** The words that I say to you I do not speak on my own authority, **but the Father who dwells in me does his works.** Believe me that I am in the Father and the Father is in me, or else believe on account of the works themselves. *"Truly, truly, I say to you, whoever believes in me will also do the works that I do; and greater works than these will he do, because I am going to the Father.*
Notice; Now the Father is abiding "with and on" Believers through the Holy Spirit and the Spirit that dwells in you **will do GOD's works through you,** just as it was with Jesus, if your Born-again Spirit lives in concert with "GOD,

the Holy Spirit"? "GOD, the Holy Spirit" will only tell you to do or say what He hears from Jesus and Father GOD. The Believer can also know what Father GOD and Jesus will say by looking at what Jesus did and said in the Bible pertaining to the new Covenant.

Remember: Jesus was conceived by the Holy Spirit and then baptized with the Holy Spirit before He did one miracle or started His ministry. Listen to the Apostle Paul tell you about the power of "GOD, the Holy Spirit" abiding inside and on each Believer that believes.

> Romans 8:11 But if **the Spirit of him that raised up Jesus from the dead dwell in you,** he that raised up Christ from the dead shall also quicken your mortal bodies by his Spirit that dwelleth in you.

Resurrection power is available to Believers Baptized with "GOD, the Holy Spirit" when there is a relationship and communication with GOD.

Question?
Jesus was conceived of the Holy Spirit,
why would Jesus need to be baptized
with the Holy Spirit?

Listen as the Angel of the Lord speaks to Joseph about Jesus and the conception of Mary his wife.

> Matthew 1:20 But as he considered these things, behold, an angel of the Lord appeared to him in a dream, saying, "Joseph, son of David, do not fear to take Mary as your wife, **for that which is**

conceived in her is from the Holy Spirit. She will bear a son, and you shall call his name Jesus, for he will save his people from their sins."
Do you realize the baptism with "GOD, the Holy Spirit" will bring to all Believers the same person of the Godhead that was on Jesus Christ at His baptism? Think about allowing "GOD, the Holy Spirit" to confirm thoughts and actions inside you. Listen to Jesus (in John 5) talk about living daily by the plan of GOD, depending on GOD's Spirit doing what he sees the Father do.

The Authority of the Son
John 5:19 So Jesus said to them,
"Truly, truly, I say to you,
>> the Son can do nothing of his own accord,
>>> **but only what he sees the Father doing.**
>>> For whatever the Father does,
>>> **that the Son does likewise.**
>> For the Father loves the Son and
> **shows him all that he himself is doing.**
>> And **greater works than these**
>>> **will he show him,**
>>>> so that you may marvel.
>> For as the **Father raises the dead**
> and gives them life,
>>> so also the **Son gives life**
>>> **to whom he will.**
>>>> The Father judges no one, but
>>> **has given all judgment to the Son,**
>> that all may honor the Son,

God, the Holy Spirit, 139

just as they honor the Father.
                Whoever does not honor the Son
                        does not honor the Father who sent him.
Believers have an account of what Jesus did while He was on Earth and therefore Believers have an account of what Father GOD did in Heaven, so when Believers are doing what Jesus did, we are doing what the Father in Heaven approved doing. **When Believers are <u>not doing</u> what Jesus did, we have no idea if we are doing something approved of by GOD?** So, go and do good deeds Jesus did, with confidence in the name of the Lord Jesus, knowing that good deeds Jesus did are approved by the Father. In the same manner any communication received from "GOD, the Holy Spirit" that is consistent with GOD's word and exemplified by Jesus actions should be assumed as proper actions for Believers to do.

The Journey to discover "GOD, the Holy Spirit".

Chapter 6

The Holy Spirit of Jesus Christ
Has been given a "bad rap" by the church.

Many Churches teach that you received "GOD, the Holy Spirit" when you believed and there is evidence that the Holy Spirit was given as a seal for the New Creation Born-again Spirit in Believers, but that does not explain all the scripture. There is also a large body of teaching and scripture that Believers can and should be Baptized into "GOD, the Holy Spirit" and the Holy Spirit can be "in and on" Believers. Scripture reveals three baptisms; Baptized into repentance from "dead Works", Baptized into Jesus Christ for redemption and sealed with "GOD, the Holy Spirit" and third Baptized with "GOD, the Holy Spirit".

The larger question than the theology of the Baptisms is, do Believers believe they received "GOD, the Holy Spirit" as a seal to their salvation, when they were saved?

- Are you talking to and listening to "GOD, the Holy Spirit" constantly?
- *is there evidence that the Believer has "GOD, the Holy Spirit" in or on the Believer?*

If there is no evidence of a moment by moment relationship with "GOD, the Holy Spirit", Believers should ask Father GOD for the Holy Spirit, so that you will know for certain that you have the Holy Spirit inside you and can start communicating with the Holy Spirit of GOD, right now. Listen to the promise of GOD.

Luke 11:13 If you then, who are evil, know how to give good gifts to your children, **how much more will the heavenly Father give the Holy Spirit to those who ask him!"**
Believers cannot be hurt by using this scripture and beginning to relate to "GOD, the Holy Spirit" right now. The Holy Spirit is a spirit personification of God. Think about this; the name of the Holy Spirit is **not Holy Spirit; the Trinity is GOD, the Father, GOD, the Son, and "GOD, the Holy Spirit"**. The Holy Spirit's name is GOD.

A new paradigm has been set in motion by the Lord's death and resurrection, Jesus Christ has given His Spirit to be inside every Believer who asks. If you want to know the will of GOD for yourself, then get to know GOD through the Holy Spirit, that is inside you. **"GOD, the Holy Spirit" is a comforter available to live inside Believers, who ask.**

Is the Holy Spirit "the GOD" you do not know?

Is the Holy Spirit, a GOD, you do not know? **Jesus did not do one miracle or start His ministry until "GOD, the Holy Spirit" was sent from Father GOD to be on and in Jesus Christ at His baptism.**

There appears to be a biblical difference in salvation and being sealed by "GOD, the Holy Spirit" and being **baptized in "GOD, the Holy Spirit". Here is a logical question;** If Jesus was created by the Holy Spirit as was told to Joseph, the husband of Mary the mother of Jesus, **why was Jesus baptized with the Holy Spirit at His baptism and why had Jesus not performed one miracle before His Baptism**

with "GOD, the Holy Spirit"?
Therefore, we can see that Jesus is from "GOD, the Holy Spirit" and yet we know Jesus Christ was also baptized with "GOD, the Holy Spirit" and we know that Jesus baptizes with "GOD, the Holy Spirit" and fire. So, there are a number of scriptures to download and explore.

Now let us fast forward to the Apostle Peter's famous sermon at Pentecost. It is evident by scripture that the disciples and 3,000 on the night of Pentecost received, **salvation, water baptism,** and **Baptism in the Holy Spirit.** What are Believers to take away from this double dose of the Holy Spirit and is there any biblical corroboration for or the need for additional power from a double dose of the Holy Spirit in the Bible? The answer is yes. Let us start with the words of John the Baptist in his daily sermon to thousands of people.

> Matthew 3:11 "I baptize you with water for repentance, but he who is coming after me is mightier than I, whose sandals I am not worthy to carry. **He will baptize you with the Holy Spirit and fire.**

Listen now to the words of Jesus at the Feast of Tabernacles ceremony; the prayer for water signified with the Golden laver of water, and the connection to the Spirit.

> **John 7:37-39** On the last day of the feast, the great day, Jesus stood up and cried out, "If anyone thirsts, let him come to me and drink. Whoever believes in me, as the Scripture has said, 'Out of his heart will flow rivers of living

water.'" **Now this he said about the Spirit,** whom **those who believed in him** were to receive, for as yet the Spirit had not been given, **because Jesus was not yet glorified.**

Notice: another proof that the Holy Spirit is given to the Believers after the Lord's resurrection and ascension.

Is there biblical evidence that the Disciples and followers were blessed with a Baptism in the Holy Spirit **after they were saved** and received the seal of their salvation, "GOD, the Holy Spirit"? **The answer is yes.** In the upper room, the first evening after resurrection, Jesus sealed His follower's salvation with the Holy Spirit. (Disciples and 120 followers)

> John 20:22   And when Jesus had said this, he breathed on them and said to them, **"Receive the Holy Spirit".**

39 days later just before the Lord ascended into Heaven, Jesus said to the Disciples, go to Jerusalem and stay until the Holy Spirit has come upon you and given you power.

> Luke 24:49   And behold, I am sending **the promise** of my Father upon you. But stay in the city until you are clothed with power from on high."

> Acts 1:8   But you will receive power when the Holy Spirit has come upon you, and you will be my witnesses in Jerusalem and in all Judea and Samaria, and to the end of the earth."

Question: Did you see, the Holy Spirit was given as a seal in John 20:22 and then Baptized with "GOD, the Holy Spirit" in Luke and Acts many times.

Note: **There is confirmation of Baptism "in and on" Believers with "GOD, the Holy Spirit".** "GOD, the Holy Spirit" seals the Believers salvation and its benefits, and the Believer can ask and be Baptized into "GOD, the Holy Spirit" which seems to be an anointing. Luke 24:49, Acts 1:8, Acts 2:16-18 and more.

Apostle Peter's Sermon on Pentecost

On Pentecost, the Apostle Peter's sermon and the Holy Spirit saw 3,000 people saved, baptized in water, and baptized in "GOD, the Holy Spirit". Listen to the Apostle Peter's sermon at the Feast of Pentecost.

Acts 2:16-18   But this is what was uttered through the **prophet Joel:** "'And in the last days it shall be, God declares, that **I will pour out my Spirit** on all flesh, and your sons and your daughters **shall prophesy,** and your young men shall see visions, and your old men shall dream dreams; even on my male servants and female servants in those days I will pour out my Spirit, and **they shall prophesy.**

Acts 2:21-23 And it shall come to pass that everyone who calls upon the name of the Lord shall be saved.' "Men of Israel, hear these words: Jesus of Nazareth, a man attested to you by God with mighty works and wonders and signs that God did through him in your midst, as you yourselves know— this Jesus, delivered up according to the definite plan and foreknowledge of God, you crucified and killed by the hands of lawless men.

Act 2:32-33 This Jesus God raised up, and of that we all are witnesses. Being therefore exalted at the right hand of God, and **having received from the Father the promise of the Holy Spirit, he has poured out this that you yourselves are seeing and hearing.**

Acts 2:38 And Peter said to them, "Repent and be baptized every one of you in the name of Jesus Christ for the forgiveness of your sins, **and you will receive the gift of the Holy Spirit.**

Acts 2:41 So those who received his word were baptized, and there were added that day about three thousand souls.

Acts 2:1-8 When the day of Pentecost arrived, they were all together in one place. And suddenly there came from heaven a sound like a mighty rushing wind, and it filled the entire house where they were sitting. And divided tongues as of fire appeared to them and rested on each one of them. **And they were all filled with the Holy Spirit and began to speak in other tongues as the Spirit gave them utterance.** Now there were dwelling in Jerusalem Jews, devout men from every nation under heaven. And at this sound the multitude came together, and they were bewildered, because each one was hearing them speak in his own language. And they were amazed and astonished, saying, "Are not all these who are speaking Galileans? And how is it that we hear, each of us in his own native language?

Scriptural History in Acts
Of the Baptism in the Holy Spirit.

All through the New Testament there are scriptures declaring Believers in Jesus Christ can be and should be Baptized in "GOD, the Holy Spirit" and with "GOD, the Holy Spirit".
Baptism in "GOD, the Holy Spirit" is verified all through the first church for many years. In Acts 2 we have the first baptism in "GOD, the Holy Spirit", three thousand were saved, and baptized in water, and baptized in "GOD, the Holy Spirit". In acts 8:14-15 (5 years later) we have a second picture of being baptized with the Holy Spirit, in Acts 10:44-48 (10 years later) another example of being baptized in "GOD, the Holy Spirit" and in Acts 19:1-6 another baptism in the Holy Spirit, (25 years later). The baptism in the Holy Spirit is needed for Believers and is happening long after the disciples have gone and in places that the disciples are not present. **Do not fall prey to religious teaching that the Baptism in "GOD, the Holy Spirit" and the miracles of GOD have gone away with the death of the disciples.** Remember that, "GOD is the same yesterday, today, and forever" and the word Disciples is not used after the Lord's ascension to Heaven, because we are now taught by "GOD, the Holy Spirit" from inside Believers. Don't allow the stories of the Baptism in "GOD, the Holy Spirit" to allow fear to invade your thoughts about the Holy Spirit.

God, the Holy Spirit, 147

Author's note: I spent thirty years in the Baptist Church and do not recall ever being taught lessons on "GOD, the Holy Spirit", so I have spent the past three years learning and writing what the Bible says to Believers about "GOD, the Holy Spirit". Everything about "GOD, the Holy Spirit" is for the Believers benefit and comfort. Think about it, Jesus has sent a comforter to be in and on Believers for your benefit. Do not allow the stigma given to "speaking in tongues" to keep you from living in constant contact with "GOD, the Holy Spirit".

"GOD, the Holy Spirit" is not weird, don't think you are going to lose control of your mouth and speak in tongues. Believers have a free will and "GOD, the Holy Spirit" will not override your decision to choose your words and actions. If you speak in an unknown language it will be "OK". Scripture says, that if we pray <u>without understanding</u> Believers are praying from our Spirit and praying in the Spirit builds Believers up. Listen to the Apostle Paul.

> **Jude 1:20** But ye, beloved, building up yourselves on your most holy faith, praying in the Holy Spirit,
> **1st Corinthians 14:14-18** For if I pray in an unknown tongue, my spirit prays, but my understanding is unfruitful. What is it then? I will pray with the spirit, and I will pray with the understanding also: I will sing with the spirit, and I will sing with the understanding also. Else when thou shalt bless with the spirit, how shall he that occupies the room of the unlearned say Amen at thy giving of thanks, seeing he understands not

what you are saying? For thou verily give thanks well, but the other is not edified. I thank my God, **I speak with tongues more than ye all: (this is a prayer language that the one offering the prayer does not understand)** God looks on the heart and whatever sounds are made, if they are given as praise to GOD, GOD will interpret. "GOD, the Holy Spirit" is always on-time, appropriate, discerning, and **will not** make you feel uncomfortable, <u>but with the Holy Spirit, you will feel like a blanket of love has wrapped you up and you know you are never alone.</u> Remember; "GOD, the Holy Spirit" is a comforter not a disrupter. The scripture does say that zeal for the Lord follows receiving the Holy Spirit of Jesus Christ and Father GOD.

What is your current position with regard to measuring your relationship with "GOD, the Holy Spirit"? **There are 10,080 minutes in a week, how many of those minutes do you spend thinking about GOD, loving God, speaking to GOD, and listening to GOD?** Do you know and talk to "GOD, the Holy Spirit" inside you hourly, daily, or weekly? The Apostle John tells Believers, that the Spirit of GOD inside Believers, is greater than the devil, who is in the world. It is imperative that Believers communicate with "GOD, the Holy Spirit". Consider this verse;

> Little children, you are from God and have overcome them (the enemy), **for he (GOD) who is in you (Believers) is greater than he (Devil) who is in the world.** They (unbelievers) are from the world; therefore, they speak from the world,

and the world listens to them. **We are from God.** Whoever knows God listens to (Believers) us; whoever is not from God does not listen to us. **By this we (Believers) know the Spirit of truth and the spirit of error.** 1st John 4:4

The last sentence informs Believers that, with "GOD, the Holy Spirit" inside, Believers, we will know the difference between the **Spirit of GOD** and the spirit of error and are guaranteed victory over the enemy. Just imagine; Jesus is the truth and has sent Believers the Spirit of Truth. This is just one of the scriptures that will help you stay out of the ditch of despair, by communicating with "GOD, the Holy Spirit". Believers must capture every thought and bring it to the Spirit of Truth to thwart the spirit of error. You may be thinking, I do not have time to ask the Holy Spirit before acting or speaking. Let me assure you that at the moment of an emotional response to a word or action, "GOD, the Holy Spirit"- in the twinkling of an eye **can lead you to not act out of anger.**

Jesus, our first comforter, will ask GOD
To send Believers another comforter,
the Holy Spirit of Jesus Christ.

Listen to Jesus at the Last Supper, talk about the importance of the Lord (in Human form) going to Heaven and the sending of "GOD, the Holy Spirit" (in Spirit form) for the benefit of billions of Christians to enable GOD to have a personal relationship with every Believer. Many denominations and churches keep GOD in Heaven and do not believe there is an active "GOD, the Holy Spirit"

God, the Holy Spirit, 150

available for Believers on earth right now, but scripture says that is a lie.

John 14:16 And I will ask the Father, and he will give you another Helper (Holy Spirit), to be with you forever, even the Spirit of truth, whom the world cannot receive, because it neither sees him nor knows him. **You know him, for he dwells "with you" and "will be in" you.**

John 14:26 But the Helper, the Holy Spirit, whom the Father will send in my name, **he will teach you all things and bring to your remembrance all that I have said to you.**

Notice: Jesus is saying, GOD will send Believers another comforter meaning that Jesus was the first comforter, for **Jesus is truth, and the comforter is the Spirit of truth.** "GOD, the Holy Spirit" will be able to teach Believers things Jesus could not teach, because Jesus had not gone to the cross and been resurrected. Believers could not be reconciled to GOD until the death and resurrection of Jesus had taken place. Now listen as Jesus tells Believers what "GOD, the Holy Spirit" will do and not do;

John 16:7 Nevertheless, I tell you the truth: **it is to your advantage that I go away,** for if I do not go away, **the Helper (Holy Spirit) will not come** to you. But if I go, I will send him to you.

And when he ("GOD, the Holy Spirit") comes, The Holy Spirit will convict the world concerning **sin** and **righteousness** and **judgment.**

- concerning **sin,** because they do not believe in me;

God, the Holy Spirit, 151

(conviction of sin is for unbelievers)

- concerning **righteousness,** because I go to the Father, and you will see me no longer; (revealing the righteousness of Jesus and salvation for Believers to promote right living)
- concerning **judgment,** because the ruler of this world is judged. (Satan no longer can accuse the Believers in the presence of GOD; his power is gone and now he can only lie.) John 16:11-13

It is very important that Believers understand the gift of "GOD, the Holy Spirit" and "GOD, the Holy Spirit" actions on earth.

- If you are an unbeliever, the Holy Spirit is here to convict you of your sin (unbelief in Jesus Christ as Savior.)
- **If you are a Believer in Jesus Christ,** the Holy Spirit is here to point you to your right-standing with GOD through Jesus Christ. Remember; GOD is remembering your sins no longer. Right living (or living holy) will only come from right believing in GOD and not from behavior modification.
- The devil has been judged and stripped of his power.

It is important to know; that **"GOD, the Holy Spirit" is not in the Believers life to point out sin,** pointing out sin was the purpose of the law, but "GOD, the Holy Spirit" is with the Believer to point the Believer to the righteousness of the Savior in the heart of the Believer. Acts of evil, works of the flesh, or lawlessness done by Believers leaves deep scars from the consequences of man-made actions but will not separate you from the Love of GOD.

After you are saved, you are not judged for performance but for your relationship with GOD. Remember the story of King David, a flawed man, whose love relationship with GOD was valuable to GOD, because the relationship represented faith and was counted as righteousness for GOD's salvation. Think about the love of GOD for mankind in this next scripture.

> **Galatians 4:3 God sent forth his Son, born of woman, born under the law, to redeem those who were under the law, so that we might receive adoption as sons. And because you are sons, God has sent the Spirit of his Son into our hearts, crying, "Abba! Father!"** So you are no longer a slave, **but a son, and if a son, then an heir through God.**

This scripture gives Believers a picture of, "what GOD thinks about believers?". **You are now part of GOD's family and you are an heir to the estate of Jesus Christ.** Imagine what an heir of GOD Almighty means to Believers and means to GOD? Build an image of Almighty GOD, as Father GOD. Imagine your Father GOD sending Believers the Spirit of His Son, "GOD, the Holy Spirit". Believers are part of GOD's family and Jesus is your big Brother and "GOD, the Holy Spirit" is your friend, that is more loyal than a brother. Christianity is about relationship with GOD **not** living the mechanics of a set of rules or patterns. The old covenant has been replaced and now Jesus has finished the New Covenant and given Believers the victory and all the spoils and trophies.

Take a minute to think about this statement: Christ has redeemed Believers from the curse of not being able to keep the law. Believers must leave performance-based religion in exchange for belief-based love for GOD and our neighbors. Religion sets up "to do" hurdles to jump over to deserve GOD to move for your requests. GOD does not have hurdles for Believers to jump except to believe GOD loved the world and sent His Son to save the world.
Listen to the next question; When you came to Jesus to exchange your signature for Jesus to sit on the throne of your life; were you without sin, were you tithing, were you loving your neighbor, were you praying, or did you have anything of value to deserve the Lord's sacrifice or **did you believe you needed a Savior and you asked Jesus into your heart with your words and belief in your heart that Jesus was your Savior, and you were saved?** Can you see the true Nature of GOD, is grace and love for Believers, without work on your part to deserve salvation through Jesus Christ?
Belief in Father GOD and his Creation, Jesus Christ and His redemption, and "GOD, the Holy Spirit" and His comfort and power is the Believers part and grace upon grace for you is GOD's part. There is no pathway for your goodness or accomplishments to get GOD to act in your behalf, just believe that GOD loves you so much that He sacrificed His Son for you and allow that love to change your heart.
Believers who came to GOD, without anything of value, to

get saved, find Churches, <u>with good intentioned people,</u> who think that anything further in the relationship with GOD <u>needs good works and holiness.</u> **That is wrong on every level,** GOD loves you so much that if you love GOD and have a preeminent relationship with "GOD, the Holy Spirit" living in your inner sanctum with your Born-again Spirit and believe GOD sent Jesus for you, ask what you will and it will be done. Miracles galore.

"GOD, the Holy Spirit" has limitless resources.

God, the Holy Spirit, 156

The Journey to discover "GOD, the Holy Spirit"

Chapter 7

How do Believers interact with "GOD, the Holy Spirit"?

This chapter is almost all scripture with comments to high-lite what the Apostle Paul and Jesus are telling us about communicating and living in the will of GOD and simultaneously living in the Kingdom of GOD through interaction with "GOD, the Holy Spirit". The overriding promise from Jesus is chronicled in this scripture.
In that day you will know that I am in my Father, and you in me, and I in you. Whoever has my (instructions) commandments and keeps them, he it is who loves me. **And he who loves me will be loved by my Father, and I will love him and manifest myself to him." John 14:21**
Note: Jesus said all through his ministry, "If you love me, keep my words". John 8:51, 14:23, 14:24, 15:20, and 1st John 2:5. Do not be thrown off by the word commandments, the word principles or my words would be better translation in this context. The Patriarchs of the Bible who loved GOD with all their heart, soul, mind, and strength found right-standing with GOD.
This incredible scripture above, is asking Believers "do we know GOD?", do we believe GOD loved us and sent Jesus to die for Believers , do we believe that Believers are in GOD and that Father GOD, Jesus the Redeemer, and "God, the Holy Spirit" will manifest Himself to be in and

on Believers. This is not a relationship of two hours on Sunday but a total emersion in GOD.

Think about what an intense relationship with "GOD, the Holy Spirit" delivers to the Believers life.

- Secret wisdom from God can only be revealed through "GOD, the Holy Spirit" for our glory.
- Jesus only did what he saw His Father do and only said what he heard His Father say.
- GOD the Holy Spirit will only declare to Believers what GOD has said and what GOD wants Believes to do.
- Jesus speaking, all that the Father has is mine; therefore, I said that "GOD, the Holy Spirit" will take what is mine and **declare it to you.**
- And Believers who love me will be loved by my Father, and I will love him **and manifest myself to them."**

Think about Jesus manifesting Himself to Believers, the definition in Strong's Dictionary of the word, manifest; is to exhibit in person, declare with words, declare plainly. These words should give you confidence to expect interaction from "GOD, the Holy Spirit" in your daily life, moment by moment.

Wisdom and power from the Spirit

1st Corinthians 2:1-5 Dear brothers and sisters, when I came to you, I told you the secret truth of God. But I did not use fancy words or great wisdom. I decided that while I was with you I would forget about everything except Jesus Christ and his death on the cross. When I came to you,

I was weak and shook with fear. My teaching and my speaking were not with wise words that persuade people. But the proof of **my teaching was the power that the Spirit gives.** I did this so that your faith would be in God's power, not in human wisdom.

Believers must reach into the Spiritual world, where GOD's word rules and the Lord's principles are mightier than the sword.

Verses 6-8 Yet among the mature we do impart wisdom, although it is not a wisdom of this age or of the rulers of this age, who are doomed to pass away. **But we impart (speak) a secret and hidden wisdom of God, which God decreed before the ages for our glory.** None of the rulers of this age understood this (that Jesus was the Messiah), for if they had, they would not have crucified the Lord of glory.

Verses 9-12 But, as it is written, **"What no eye has seen, nor ear heard, nor the heart of man imagined, what God has prepared for those who love him"—these things God has revealed to us through the Spirit.** For the Spirit searches everything, even the depths of God. For who knows a person's thoughts except the spirit of that person, which is in him? So also no one comprehends the thoughts of God except the Spirit of God. **Now we have received not the spirit of the world, but the Spirit who is from God, that we might understand the things freely**

given us by God.
Read these verses several times to see the power inside Believers, a power we must embrace and couple with a relationship with "GOD, the Holy Spirit" for the fulfillment of GOD's word for the benefit of others.

>**Verses 13-16 And we impart this in words not taught by human wisdom but taught by the Spirit,** interpreting spiritual truths to those who are spiritual. The natural person does not accept the things of the Spirit of God, for they are folly to him, and he is not able to understand them because they are spiritually discerned. **The spiritual person judges all things,** but is himself to be judged by no one. "For who has understood the mind of the Lord so as to instruct him?" **But we (Believers) have the mind of Christ.**

Can you even fathom that Believers have the "Mind of Christ" (the intellect of Jesus)? What are we to do with this truth? Answer: Judge all thoughts before letting a thought of evil, influence a Believer to act out of an emotion of anger or revenge, etc. instead of love. Believers must relate to and speak to "GOD, the Holy Spirit" inside Believers all the time depending on the mind of Christ for leadership.

The Authority of the Son
Think about the Lord's life; He saved, healed, delivered, and provided what people needed, and scripture says He did not do anything He did not see the Father do. Jesus has said, that "GOD, the Holy Spirit" will only tell Believers

what He hears from the Father and the Son.

John 5:19-29 So Jesus said to them, "Truly, truly, I say to you, the Son can do nothing of his own accord, **but only what he sees the Father doing.** For whatever the Father does, **that the Son does likewise.** For the Father loves the Son and <u>shows him all that he himself is doing.</u> **And greater works than these will he show him, so that you may marvel.** For as the Father raises the dead and gives them life, so also the Son gives life to whom he will. The Father judges no one, but has given all judgment to the Son, <u>that all may honor the Son, just as they honor the Father.</u> **Whoever does not honor the Son does not honor the Father who sent him.** Truly, truly, I say to you, whoever hears my word and believes him who sent me has eternal life.** He does not come into judgment, but has passed from death to life.

The Bible and especially the books written about the new covenant that was delivered to Believers at the cross are a picture of what GOD is doing in Heaven and what he wants us to do on earth.

John 8:28-29 So Jesus said to them, "When you have lifted up the Son of Man, then you will know that I am he, and **that I do nothing on my own authority, but speak just as the Father taught me.** And he who sent me is with me. He has not left me alone, **for I always do the things that are pleasing to him."**

It is important to build on the fact that Jesus did, what He saw the Father do and Jesus has sent "GOD, the Holy Spirit" to show Believers what he sees Father GOD and Jesus do and say. Believers are the Ambassadors for Jesus Christ led to act by "GOD the Holy Spirit" to do great works the Father will show you.

John 14:10 Do you not believe that I am in the Father and the Father is in me? **The words that I say to you I do not speak on my own authority, but the Father who dwells in me does his works. The Great Commission of Jesus;** Go everywhere in the world. Tell the Good News to everyone. **Whoever believes and is baptized will be saved.** But those who do not believe will be judged guilty. **And the people who believe will be able to do these things as proof:** They will use my name to force demons out of people. They will speak in languages they never learned. If they pick up snakes or drink any poison, they will not be hurt. They will lay their hands on sick people, and they will get well." After the Lord Jesus said these things to his followers, he was carried up into heaven. There, Jesus sat at the right side of God. **The followers went everywhere in the world telling people the Good News, and the Lord helped them. By giving them power to do miracles the Lord proved that their message was true.** Mark 16:16-20 ERV.

Father GOD and Jesus Christ have not changed and "GOD, the Holy Spirit" has not changed; GOD who created the world and Jesus who redeemed the world

and "GOD, the Holy Spirit" who is "in and on" Believers baptized with the Holy Spirit is ready to couple with Believers to do the mighty works of The Father to answer prayers of the Saints and give revelation to the unbeliever.

Jesus, at the Last Supper declares this verse;

> John 16:12-15 **"I still have many things to say to you,** but you cannot bear them now. **When the Spirit of truth comes, he will guide you into all the truth, for he will not speak on his own authority, but whatever he hears he will speak, and he will declare to you the things that are to come.** He will glorify me, **for he will take what is mine and declare it to you.** All that the Father has is mine; therefore I said that he will take what is mine and **declare it to you.**

Can you see the development of the power of the New Covenant building and the Believers need to bust down the door to the Spiritual world and be ready to do the great works of GOD that Father GOD will do through you?

Believers can expect, if you and your Spirit are listening, "GOD, the Holy Spirit" will give you words to say and the Father will do His amazing works through you. **Jesus is finished,** no longer available in the flesh on Earth; it is now the Believers turn to be a steward of all that GOD has given you for the benefit of others. Take a minute to contemplate this thought.

> **1st Peter 2:9** But ye are a chosen generation, a royal priesthood, an holy nation, a peculiar

people; that ye should shew forth the praises of him who hath called you out of darkness into his marvelous light: Which in time past were not a people, but *are* now the people of God: which had not obtained mercy, but now have obtained mercy.

Peter closes the chapter with this promise:

1st Peter 2:24-25 He himself bore our sins in his body on the tree, that we might die to sin and live to righteousness. By his wounds you have been healed. For you were straying like sheep, but have now returned to the Shepherd and Overseer of your souls.

Jesus Promises the Holy Spirit
so that you do not have to be alone or act alone.

John 14:15-31 "If you love me, you will keep my (Precepts) commandments. And I will ask the Father, and he will give you another Helper, to be with you forever, **even the Spirit of truth,** whom the world cannot receive, because it neither sees him nor knows him. **You know him, for he dwells with you and will be in you.**

Notice: this scripture announces there are two parts to the Believers relationship with "GOD, the Holy Spirit", starting with the question; Do you love GOD? If so, "GOD, the Holy Spirit" is in you to seal your Salvation and all its benefits and **will be on you with the baptism with "GOD, the Holy Spirit".** This backs up Jesus being formed by the

Holy Spirit but also Jesus was baptized with "GOD, the Holy Spirit" before He started His ministry and the miracles accompanied His ministry. Jesus continues His discourse.

"I will not leave you as orphans; I will come to you. Yet a little while and the world will see me no more, but you will see me. Because I live, you also will live. **In that day you will know that I am in my Father, and you in me, and I in you.** Whoever has my commandments and keeps them, he it is who loves me. And he who loves me will be loved by my Father, and I will love him **and manifest myself to him."** Judas (not Iscariot) said to him, "Lord, how is it that you will manifest yourself to us, and not to the world?" Jesus answered him, **"If anyone loves me, he will keep my word, and my Father will love him, and we will come to him and make our home with him.** Whoever does not love me does not keep my words. **And the word that you hear is not mine but the Father's who sent me.** "These things I have spoken to you while I am still with you. **But the Helper, the Holy Spirit, whom the Father will send in my name, he will teach you all things and bring to your remembrance all that I have said to** you. John 14:15-26

Do you feel the love from your Savior in these verses? A Believer, who does not know the words of the Lord and the power in the New Covenant will be at a deficit to match the communication of "GOD, the Holy Spirit", from the words of GOD. Listen as Jesus gives Believers His peace.

Peace I leave with you; my peace I give to you. Not as the world gives do I give to you. Let not your hearts be troubled, neither let them be afraid. You heard me say to you, 'I am going away, and I will come to you.' **If you loved me, you would have rejoiced, because I am going to the Father, for the Father is greater than I.** And now I have told you before it takes place, so that when it does take place you may believe. John 14:27-29

Believers can rest in the new era of GOD with mankind through "GOD, the Holy Spirit", let not your heart be troubled, neither let it be afraid. Did you see the instruction for Believers to "not let your heart be troubled neither let it be afraid"?

Now listen to the Lord and see the garden of good fruit that will grow from the seeds of the words the Lord planted in your heart.

John 15:7-12 **If you abide in me, and my words abide in you, ask whatever you wish, and it will be done for you.** By this <u>my Father is glorified, that you bear much fruit</u> and so prove to be my disciples. As the Father has loved me, so have I loved you. Abide in my love. If you keep my commandments (instructions), you will abide in my love, just as I have kept my Father's commandments and abide in his love. **These** things I have spoken to you, that my joy may be in you, and that your joy may be full. **"This is my commandment,** that you love one another as I have loved you.

When you read these words from Jesus, are you concerned that His words are abiding in you? Have you received His love, and do you enjoy the Lord's joy inside your being and is your joy full?

John 16:22-23 So also you have sorrow now, but I will see you again, and your hearts will rejoice, and **no one will take your joy from you. In that day you will ask nothing of me. Truly, truly,** I say to you, **whatever you ask of the Father in my name, he will give it to you.** Until now you have asked nothing in my name. **Ask, and you will receive, that your joy may be full.** And now, Father, glorify me in your own presence with the glory that I had with you before the world existed. **"I have manifested your name to the people whom you gave me out of the world.** Yours they were, and you gave them to me, and they have kept your word. Now they know that **everything that you have given me is from you.**

Verse after verse is expressing Father GOD's and the Lord's love for Believers. It is difficult to take into our belief system, because we have lived the first part of our life loving and worshipping ourselves. Only after realizing our need for a Savior, have we considered living our life loving GOD and considering others more significantly than ourselves. **The very idea to think of GOD before we think**

God, the Holy Spirit, 167

about ourselves is not our nature as mankind and then to compound that conundrum by considering others before considering ourselves is foreign, but that is the way to GOD's life for Believers.

Are you overwhelmed, that believing Father GOD sent Jesus and Jesus sent "GOD, the Holy Spirit" is the foundation for faith that moves mountains?

> John 17:8 **For I have given them the words that you gave me,** and they have received them and have come to know in truth **that I came from you; and** they have believed that you sent me.

Notice again, the importance of believing Father GOD has sent Jesus. Not that Father GOD sent Jesus to save the world, but that Believers know and believe **Father GOD sent Jesus.**

Now another word from the Lord talking to Father GOD about you and me.

> John 17:16-23 **They are not of the world, just as I am not of the world.** Sanctify them in the truth; your word is truth. As you sent me into the world, so I have sent them into the world. **And for their sake I consecrate myself, that they also may be sanctified in truth.** "I do not ask for these only, but also for those who will believe in me through their word, **that they may all be one, just as you, Father, are in me, and I in you, that they also may be in us, so that the world may believe that you have sent me.**

Notice: the inclusion of all the Believers in the world, after Jesus, that are saved, healed, delivered, and live in peace.

Again, Jesus is saying; They have believed that **Father GOD has sent Jesus the Christ.** So that Believers might be in Father GOD and Jesus Christ, so that the world will know Father GOD has sent Jesus.

> **The glory that you have given me I have given to them, that they may be one even as we are one,** I in them and you in me, that they **may become perfectly one,** so that the world may know **that you sent me** and loved them even as you loved me.

A very important announcement: **Another proclamation that the destiny for Believers is to become perfectly one with "God, the Holy Spirit" so the world will know that Father GOD sent Jesus.**

Jesus speaking, As you sent me into the world, so I have sent them into the world. **And all the ones who believe in me through their word.** This is just another proof that miracles did not die with the Apostles but lives on through all that believe through the words and acts of Believers. **Jesus has sent Believers into the world as Jesus was sent into the world. "GOD, the Holy Spirit" is on Believers as "GOD, the Holy Spirit" was on Jesus Christ. Jesus was sent into the world, baptized in the Holy Spirit, and sends Believers into the world to be baptized in "GOD, the Holy Spirit" with power.**

> **John 7:37-39** On the last day of the feast, the great day, **Jesus** stood up and cried out, "If anyone thirsts, let him come to me and drink. Whoever believes in me, as the Scripture has said, 'Out of his heart will flow rivers of living

water.'" **Now this he said about the Spirit,** whom those who believed in him were to receive, <u>for as yet the Spirit had not been given,</u> **because Jesus was not yet glorified.**
What a wonderful Savior!

The Journey to discover "GOD, the Holy Spirit".

Chapter 8

There are consequences
to every word and action
that are not part of God's plan.

Right living cannot be accomplished **without right believing** and wrong living is established from wrong believing. Listen to the Apostle Paul describe the degrading of life by wrong believing.

> Romans 1:20 There are things about God that people cannot see—his eternal power and all that makes him God. But since the beginning of the world, those things have been easy for people to understand. They are made clear in what God has made. **So, people have no excuse for the evil they do.** People knew God, **but they did not honor him as God, and they did not thank him.** Their ideas were all useless. There was not one good thought left in their foolish minds. They said they were wise, but they became fools. Instead of honoring the divine greatness of God, who lives forever, they traded it for the worship of idols—things made to look like humans, who get sick and die, or like birds, animals, and snakes. People wanted only to do evil. So God left them and let them go their sinful way. And so they became completely immoral and used their

bodies in shameful ways with each other. **They traded the truth of God for a lie.** They bowed down and worshiped the things God made instead of worshiping the God who made those things. **He is the one who should be praised forever.** Amen.

Believers must understand your personal evil actions do not send you to hell, **unbelief** in Jesus Christ as your Savior and your inherent need for GOD in your life sends you to hell. For Unbelievers, **Not** turning your life from selfcentered to GOD-centered results in living in idolatry and abandoning the truth that is, "GOD and His Creation". Not honoring GOD for who he is and His son for what He did to redeem mankind will cause your name to be blotted out of the "Lambs book of Life".

Once unbelievers deny the existence of GOD and cover their need for GOD with wrong living you become addicted to idolatry of self-determination. How do you recover without a GOD?

A picture of sowing the spiritual word
In your heart

Acts 20:32 And now, brethren, **I commend you to God, and to the word of his grace, which is able to build you up,** and **to give you an inheritance** among all them which are sanctified.

Isaiah 55:10 "For as the rain and the snow come down from heaven and do not return there but water the earth, making it bring forth and sprout,

giving seed to the sower and bread to the eater, so shall my word be that goes out from my mouth; it shall not return to me empty, **but it shall accomplish that which I purpose, and shall succeed in the thing for which I sent it.**
John 6:27 Do not work for the food that perishes, but for the food that endures to eternal life, which the Son of Man will give to you. For on him God the Father has set his seal." Then they said to him, "What must we do, to be doing the works of God?" Jesus answered them, "This is the work of God, **that you believe in him whom he has sent."**

Your daily walk to be holy (set apart to GOD) is to reposition your mind to agree with your Spirit to receive what God has already finished and Believers have inherited.

- Believers must believe in Jesus, whom GOD sent for Believers redemption and right standing with GOD.
- Believers have to move ourselves into position to combine our renewed mind and our redeemed spirit in concert with "GOD, the Holy Spirit".
- Faith does not cause a positive response from GOD, GOD and Jesus have already **finished** and stored up for Believers, whatever grace you're asking GOD to produce.
- GOD, at creation, made enough air to breathe, food to eat, water to drink, beauty to see, sounds to hear for the entire world.

• Jesus Christ has reconciled Believers to GOD, paid for all sin, and GOD is merciful to Believers lawlessness. Jesus packed Believers Born-again spirit with fruit, sent the Holy Spirit for comfort, power, revelation, and to show you things to come.

To the Believer, all of GOD's blessings and the blessings from Jesus **are outside time, ages old, and must be appropriated by belief, faith, and love in your heart.** If you think you are saved, you must realize that your Lord died 1992 years ago and was raised for your salvation and all the benefits of salvation. **It did not happen when you ask the Lord to sit on the "Throne of your life"; you just believed in your need for a Savior and GOD allowed you to see and understand that GOD's gift of His son and the gift of the Holy Spirit has been stored up for Believers waiting on you to give voice to your need.** The Believers name was already written in "The Lambs book of Life" entered at the Lord's resurrection. The only way to have your name removed from the, "Lambs book of Life" is to not believe in your need for a savior on the "Throne of your Life", at which time your name will be blotted out of the book.

Revelation 3:5 The one who conquers will be clothed thus in white garments, and **I will never blot his name out of the book of life.** I will confess his name before my Father and before his angels.

Loving yourself more than you love GOD will cause you name to be blotted out of the "Lambs Book of Life".

God, the Holy Spirit, 174

What are the benefits of Salvation
and what are not?

You cannot use your faith to reposition yourself to obtain *what GOD's grace has not made available.*

God **has not made** available wealth for you, for storing up in barns.

God **has not made** available another spouse for the pleasure of sex.

God **has not made** time for idle or injurious talk.

GOD **has not made** devious lifestyle a pathway to success.

GOD's grace has made the following benefits to salvation available to Believers as an inheritance from Jesus Christ and given Believers "GOD, the Holy Spirit" to be your executor of your inheritance.

God **has made** available healing for your bodies by the stripes on his body.

Grace and peace **grow** with the knowledge of GOD

God **has made** available all things needed for the life and Godliness.

God **has made** the home of the upright to flourish.

God **has made** good men to be filled with the fruit of his ways.

God **has given** long life to those who honor their parents.

GOD **has given** His Spirit to all those who ask.

GOD **has given** His world to Believers to steward.

GOD **has given** Believers acts of kindness to do.

Acts of kindness store up blessings in Heaven and bring glory to our Lord.

When, as a Believer, you are **not living** the abundant life

Jesus gave Believers; the Believer must **STOP; evaluate their current position and change their thinking according to scripture.** Depend on your relationship with "GOD, the Holy Spirit", the renewal of your mind to the truth of GOD's word, and your identity as a Child of GOD with resurrection power. If Believers are down, depressed, downtrodden, then Believers are not understanding what Christ has done for you at the Cross. Plant scriptures of the Lord's peace given to you into your mind. **Allow your mind** to rule your senses and activate your brain to use the created brain mindsets of what Jesus has promised Believers to control your body and your life issues. 2nd Timothy 1:7, 2nd Peter 5:7

If Believers need healing, Believers need to hear the word of GOD on healing and develop mindsets in your brain which produce proteins that have energy to complete their content. Then when your mind of Christ sends commands to your brain, the mind can use the mindsets of healing to cause the body to function properly.

If Believers need provision, Believers need to hear the word of GOD on provision and plant thoughts of provision and prosperity in your brain until you have established a mindset of GOD's desire and ability to send blessings to you until you do not have room enough to contain them.

Rejoice in the Lord always, again I will say, rejoice.
Let your reasonableness be known to everyone.
The Lord is at hand;
do not be anxious about anything,

God, the Holy Spirit, 176

but in everything by prayer
and supplication with thanksgiving
let your requests be made known to God. And
the peace of God, which surpasses all understanding,
will guard your hearts and your minds
in Christ Jesus.
Finally, brothers, whatever is true,
whatever is honorable,
whatever is just,
whatever is pure,
whatever is lovely,
whatever is commendable,
if there is any excellence,
if there is anything worthy of praise,
think about these things.
What you have learned
and received and heard
and seen in me—
practice these things, and
the God of peace will be with you.
Philippians 4:4

Notice Believers need to be nurturing, memorizing, and meditating on GOD's promises to eliminate doubt and unbelief strongholds in the Believers brain.

Galatians 6:3 For **if anyone thinks he is something,
when he is nothing, he deceives himself.**
But let each one test his own work, and
then his reason to boast

God, the Holy Spirit, 177

will be in himself alone
and not in his neighbor.
For each will have to bear his own load.
Let the one who is taught the word
share all good things with the one who teaches.
Do not be deceived: God is not mocked,
for whatever one sows,
that will he also reap.
For the one who
sows to his own flesh
will from the flesh reap corruption, but
the one who sows to the Spirit
will from the Spirit reap eternal life.
And let us **not grow weary of doing good,**
for in due season **we will reap,**
if we do not give up.
So then, as we have opportunity,
Let us do good to everyone, and especially
to those who are of the household of faith.

Psalms 71:20-25 Thy righteousness also, O God, is very high, who hast done great things: **O God, who is like unto thee!** Thou, which hast shewed me great and sore troubles, shalt quicken me again, and shalt bring me up again from the depths of the earth. Thou shalt increase my greatness, and comfort me on every side. I will also praise thee with the psaltery, even thy truth, O my God: unto thee will I sing with the harp, O thou Holy One of Israel. **My lips shall greatly rejoice when I sing unto thee; and my soul, which thou hast redeemed. My tongue also**

shall talk of thy righteousness all the day long: for they are confounded, for they are brought unto shame, that seek my hurt.

Another scripture to enforce the confidence we have in the New Covenant and how GOD changed our lives through the gift of the Holy Spirit of Jesus Christ in Believers.

2nd Corinthians 3:3 And you show that you (Believers) are a letter from Christ delivered by us,
> **written not with ink**
> > **but with the Spirit of the living God,**
> > > **not on tablets of stone**
> > **but on tablets of human hearts.**
> Such is the confidence that we have
through Christ toward God.
> Not that we are sufficient in ourselves
> > to claim anything as coming from us,
> > > **but our sufficiency is from God,**
> > **who has made us sufficient**
> > > **to be ministers**
> > > > **of a new covenant,**
> > > > > not of the letter
> > > > but of the Spirit.
> > For the letter kills,
> > > but the Spirit gives life.
> **Now if the ministry of death,**
carved in letters on stone
> > (Ten Commandments), came with such glory
> > > that the Israelites could not gaze

God, the Holy Spirit, 179

at Moses' face
because of its glory,
which was being brought
to an end,
**will not the ministry of the Spirit
have even more glory?**
For if there was gloryin the ministry of condemnation,
the **ministry of righteousness must far exceed**
(the law) it in glory. Indeed, in this case,
**what(the law) once had glory
has come to have
no glory at all,**
because of the glory
(New Covenant)
that surpasses it.
For if what was being (the law) brought to an end
came with glory, **much more
will what is permanent have glory.**
Since we have such a hope,
we are very bold,
not like Moses,
who would put a
veil over his face
so that the Israelites
might not gaze at the outcome of
what was being brought to an end.
But their minds were hardened.
For to this day, when they read
the old covenant,
that same veil remains unlifted,

God, the Holy Spirit, 180

because only through Christ is it taken away.
Yes, to this day whenever Moses is read
a veil lies over their hearts.
But when one turns to the Lord,
the veil is removed.
Now the Lord is the Spirit,
and where the Spirit of the Lord is,
there is freedom.
And we all, with unveiled face,
beholding the glory of the Lord,
are being transformed
into the same image
from one degree of glory to another.
For this comes from the Lord who is the Spirit.

This scripture gives a full profile of the life available to Believers filled with "GOD, the Holy Spirit" and concerned about others more than themselves.

Romans 11:36 For from (Jesus) and through (Jesus) and to (Jesus) are all things. To him be glory forever. Amen.

Obstacles to Right living through Right believing.

Unbelief or ignorance of GOD's word confuses the believer's faith. (Matthew 21:19-21, Mark 11:20-21) At the Fig tree experience with the Disciples, Jesus said, "have faith and not doubt in your heart", Believers cannot allow unbelief, to cloud your faith in GOD. When you speak words of life to any situation you must believe and not doubt. In Mark 9 the disciples were **not** successful in immediate deliverance of the demon from the young man and it looked like the demonic symptoms grew worse. The disciples quit and allowed unbelief to negate their faith because the demon made the situation look worse. The Disciples believed their eyes instead of their authority from the word of GOD and allowed unbelief to negate their faith. When the Disciples ask the Lord for the reason that this demon was not delivered at their spoken word the Lord said that their unbelief was the reason. When they saw the symptoms grow worse, they doubted their authority in the word of GOD. The Lord informed the Disciples that this **kind of unbelief** comes out only by prayer and fasting. Jesus was not talking about the demons but the unbelief in the Disciples authority given them by GOD.

America is a Christian nation at its roots, but unbelief has overturned the faith of the nation with division. Television and the internet have opened up man-made solutions to questions and problems, without offering GOD centered solutions or truths. Television and the internet solutions do not offer the words of life but create thoughts of unbelief against the word of GOD. Only the word of GOD can give life. Television and internet platforms are not evil of themselves but their content in general, is based on man-made knowledge and is generally against the word of GOD; electronic solutions are not based on love, which is the power to bring peace to the family and the world.

A foundational truth, Believers have been given their inheritance, from 1,992 years ago. The Believers mind can operate outside time, your mind is part of the eternal you. If your brain has mindsets of information about GOD and the gift of His Son, the Believers mind can draw from the mindset of GOD's promises. At the death and resurrection of Jesus Christ: Believers were saved, were made righteous, were healed, were redeemed, were sanctified, were made prosperous, etc. and these facts must form the foundation of the inheritance. Jesus has left for every Believer who makes a claim on their inheritance, the benefits of being a Believer and being adopted into the Family of GOD.

Jesus has given Believers "standing" to enforce the spiritual value of GOD's word to change the visible world from the Spiritual world. The word of GOD needs to be voice activated to send the TRUTH and power of GOD's words to complete what GOD designed the words to do. Do you understand; the "standing" Jesus has given Believers to use words of life to control your world in the Name of Jesus? Scripture reveals that Jesus is the high Priest of Believers confession or words spoken with "standing". The name of Jesus is not the four words to use to end a prayer; **Jesus has given Believers standing to change the world through a word from GOD spoken from a heart of love, in the Name of Jesus.**

Remember Jesus new name is King of Kings and Lord of Lords and Believers are the Kings and the Lords.

God, the Holy Spirit, 183

Listen to this verse in 1st John 4:16-18

> 1st John 4:16 And we have **known** and **believed the love that God** hath to us. God is love; and he that dwelleth in love dwelleth in God, and God in him. **Herein is our love made perfect,** that we may have boldness in the day of judgment: **because as he is, so are we in this world.** There is no fear in love; but perfect love cast out fear: because fear hath torment. He that fear is not made perfect in love.

Notice; GOD abides in you and you abide in love and are made perfect because **as Jesus is, so are Believers in this world.** Believers can change their situation by re-focusing on the Believers relationship with "GOD, the Holy Spirit". Believers are, "What GOD says you are, and not what you feel that you are".

Names and Words have power imbedded in them.

Names and words are important to GOD and should be important to Believers because GOD's word is forever.

> Proverbs 18:21 Death and life are in the power of the tongue, and those who love it will eat its fruits.

Great men and women of the Bible have been given powerful names that empowered them to fulfill their special destinies. In present times, names are given to children without prayer and without the knowledge of the meaning of the names assigned to children. The authors given names are David (A man after GOD's own heart) and Michael (the mighty angel of GOD) names that always reminded me or should have reminded me that I was meant to be a child of GOD. If your names did not reflect a biblical perspective to your name and you did not have a re-enforcing idea about GOD every time your name was mentioned, becoming a child of GOD gives you a new chance to have a new name to forever change your perspective, "you are now a child of GOD, a Believer, Jesus is your brother, and GOD is your Father.

The changing OF your name from sinner, addict, or atheist to Christian, requires a change to your heart from the idolatry of being self-centered to living in the love and grace offered by the Creator of all. Changing your heart from self-centered to GOD-centered will change your old habits and redeem your life from destruction (1st Timothy 6:9) and give you a relationship with the GOD of Creation, Jesus Christ, the Redeemer, and "GOD, the Holy Spirit". Constantly praising GOD for His creation, His redemption, and His love for Believers will change the Believers lifestyle to right living because of right believing.

The End

Contact the Author at
dmichaelcotten@att.net

Searchlight Press
Who are you looking for?
Publishers of thoughtful Christian books
since 1994.
PO Box 554
Henderson, TX 75653-0554
www.JohnCunyus.com

God, the Holy Spirit, 186